P9-AOV-734

Do Socialist Economies Work?

To Linda, with love

MICHAEL BLEANEY

Do Socialist Economies Work?

The Soviet and East European Experience

Basil Blackwell

First published 1988

Basil Blackwell Ltd
108 Cowley Road, Oxford, OX4 1JF, UK

Basil Blackwell Inc.
432 Park Avenue South, Suite 1503
New York, NY 10016, USA

British Library Cataloguing in Publication Data

Bleaney, Michael
Do socialist economies work? The Soviet and East European experience. 1. Eastern Europe & Soviet Union. Economic conditions
I. Title 330.947

ISBN 0–631–15306–3

Library of Congress Cataloging in Publication Data

Bleaney, M. F.
Do socialist economies work?: the Soviet and East European experience / Michael Bleaney.
p. cm.
Bibliography: p.
Includes index.
ISBN 0-631-15306-3
1. Central planning—Soviet Union. 2. Soviet Union—Economic policy—1917- 3. Soviet Union—Economic conditions—1918- 4. Central planning—Europe, Eastern. 5. Europe, Eastern—Economic policy. 6. Europe, Eastern—Economic conditions—1945- I. Title.
HC335.3.B57 1988
338.947—dc19 88-6374
CIP

Typeset in 10 on 12 pt Plantin by Graphicraft Typesetters Ltd., Hong Kong.
Printed in Great Britain by T.J. Press Ltd., Padstow, Cornwall.

Contents

List of Tables

Preface

Do socialist economies work? The answer is evidently yes, because otherwise they would not continue to exist. The real issue is: do they work well enough to be considered a desirable form of economic organization? This book addresses this question by examining the socialist economies of the USSR and the eastern half of Europe. These are the most advanced socialist economies in the world, which have evolved their current structure over a period of four decades in eastern Europe, and seven in the Soviet Union. They therefore provide a wealth of material for economic analysis.

Although much has been written in English on the economics of eastern Europe and the USSR, and the literature on Yugoslavia and the Soviet Union is especially large, most economists working in English-speaking countries, let alone students or committed socialists, are little acquainted with this work, either empirical or theoretical. To some extent this is because it is not easily accessible. The average economic book or journal article on eastern Europe has often seemed to be filled with details of adjustments to planning procedures and to be thin on analytical insight. In recent years, however, specialist writing has become less institutional and more theoretical, and this book could be seen as an attempt to consolidate this welcome trend. The emphasis is not on the nuts and bolts of the planning mechanism, compulsory indicators, bonus regulations and the like, but on economic behaviour under such a system of central planning. The object is to understand how enterprises react to the environment which they face, how planners deal with the limitations of their information about enterprises, and how the concerns of the political leadership influence the whole process. Throughout the book, and more especially in chapter 7, an attempt is made to link the analysis of microeconomic behaviour to macroeconomic performance as revealed in published statistics.

The book covers the USSR, Poland, the German Democratic Republic, Czechoslovakia, Romania, Bulgaria and Yugoslavia. Published information about Albania is too scanty for it to be included. Yugoslavia is treated in a separate chapter (chapter 8). The expression 'eastern Europe' is used to cover Bulgaria, Czechoslovakia, the GDR, Hungary, Poland and Romania i.e. it does *not* normally include Yugoslavia and the Soviet Union. Where the phrase 'the Soviet bloc' appears, this is synonymous with 'eastern Europe and the USSR'.

The book starts with two chapters which are broadly historical. Chapter 1 surveys the economic history of the USSR up to the outbreak of war in 1941. The intention here is not to produce a summary historical account, but to focus on certain aspects of the period which have some bearing on the subsequent discussion. One of these is agrarian relations. The historical confrontation between the world's first socialist state and an independent peasantry was resolved in a way which has exerted enormous influence on subsequent agricultural development in the USSR. Moreover, it was also a determinant influence on the agricultural policy of the eastern European countries, where in the immediate post-war years land reforms had produced a structure of landownership rather similar to that of post-revolutionary Russia. The evolution of the 1930s system of economic planning, which was imitated throughout eastern Europe in the Stalinist period and is now regarded as the 'traditional model', is of interest for the light that it sheds on current issues of economic reform. I argue that the form taken by planning was determined by more than Stalin's immediate objectives; the movement towards a fixed-price, administrative structure of planning was started much earlier in the 1920s. The final section of chapter 1 discusses the achievements of the Soviet growth effort in the 1930s, in terms of labour productivity, gross national product per capita and the proportion of resources devoted to investment and consumption.

Chapter 2 is a summary history of the post-war period in the USSR and eastern Europe, which is included primarily in order to facilitate the subsequent discussion. Growth performance is summarized in terms of official statistics on net material product per employee. What stands out is the extent to which the growth rate has tended to decelerate from one quinquennium to the next, although there has been some recovery from the exceptionally low levels of 1980–2. This chapter also contains a section on the theory of cycles in socialist economies, and ends with a review of developments in the agricultural sector.

Chapters 3 and 4 discuss the planning mechanism, the behaviour of enterprises under this mechanism and the interactions between planners and enterprises. Chapter 3 focuses mainly on what might be termed the 'static' issues of planning: how the planners can induce enterprises to produce output of the quality and in the quantity desired, and how enterprises operate in response to the rules of the game laid down by the planners. There is extensive discussion of the effects of 'partial' or 'administrative' reforms (i.e. alterations to compulsory plan indicators and the rules of bonus formation within a bureaucratic planning structure), and in particular their success in eliminating 'negative' forms of enterprise behaviour.

Chapter 4 takes up the 'dynamic' aspects of planning: investment and technical progress. It discusses the bias towards extensive investment and the reluctance of enterprises to make technical changes which devalue their investment in existing supply relationships. This chapter includes a treatment of Kornai's notion of the 'soft budget constraint', the tendency towards over-investment, and current controversies over the degree of excess demand in consumer goods markets in centrally planned economies.

With the exception of chapter 7, the rest of the book is taken up with studies of individual countries. No special chapter is devoted to the USSR, because most of the references in chapters 3 and 4 are to Soviet examples. Chapter 5 looks at the country which has undergone the deepest and most prolonged crisis ever experienced by a socialist country in peacetime: Poland. What is interesting about the Polish case is the interaction between political events and economic policy; though the party leaders clearly made major economic policy mistakes, they were driven down that road by fear of workers' reaction to alternative policies and a desperate desire to re-establish the credibility of the party. Rather little is said in this chapter about economic reform, not because of the absence of proposals or measures of this kind in Poland, but because they have been a rather minor element in the escalation of the crisis.

Chapter 6 discusses the economic reforms introduced in Hungary in 1968 under the title of the 'New Economic Mechanism'. This reform was more fundamental than those carried out elsewhere in the Soviet bloc, in dispensing with obligatory plan targets for current output, attempting to establish financial indicators as the main instrument of planning and permitting producers a significant degree of independence in price determination. The reform has certainly alleviated some of the static problems of traditional central planning, but it has achieved much less in the area of dynamics, for reasons elucidated in the chapter.

Chapter 7 attempts a wide-ranging assessment of economic performance in the socialist countries in comparison with the market economies of western Europe. Aspects of performance covered include consumer satisfaction, unemployment, income distribution, inflation and economic growth.

Chapter 8 discusses the nature of the economic system in Yugoslavia, its differences from eastern Europe and its record in practice. Yugoslavia diverged at a rather early date from the Soviet model, largely for political reasons, and in the 1960s disbanded most of the apparatus of central planning in favour of 'employee self-management'. The Yugoslav experiment has generated a great deal of international interest. Although economic performance up to 1979 seemed generally good, if not out of line with that of other south European countries, there has been a dramatic deterioration in the 1980s (to some extent foreshadowed in the 1970s) which has highlighted a range of difficulties. In fact, some of the problems of the Yugoslav economy are similar to those of the east European countries, and seem to have their root in a political commitment to insulate workers' incomes from the effects of enterprise inefficiency.

Finally, in chapter 9, I comment on the relationship between the economic characteristics of Soviet-type economies and their political system, the prospects for and resistances to major economic reforms, and the degree to which we can draw general conclusions about socialist economies from their experience. There is considerable evidence that the authorities in the Soviet bloc now share the widespread western opinion that their economies leave much to be desired, particularly in the field of technical progress. Though slow growth may be tolerable for a while, its longer-term effect is to undermine the international position of the country and indeed the political credibility of the leadership. It will be extremely interesting to see just how the Communist Parties go about meeting this challenge.

1

The Formation of the Soviet Economic System

Introduction

Until 1917 the economics of socialism was a purely theoretical issue. In October of that year, the Bolshevik revolution brought to power a government determined to make it a practical matter. The circumstances were hardly propitious. Lenin and his followers found themselves in charge of a semi-developed economy that was on the verge of collapse. About this they had few illusions; they pinned their hopes on the European revolution, which they expected their action to spark off. Had such a pan-European revolution occurred, the history of the socialist movement would have been very different; but in their frantic attempts to provoke it, the Bolsheviks succeeded only in bringing about a profound split in the movement, of which the Communist section henceforth owed unswerving allegiance to the USSR.

The isolation of the Russian revolution, the lessons which its leaders chose to draw from the revolutionary experience (especially the alleged superiority of Soviets over parliamentary democracy), and the backwardness and lack of democratic traditions in the country conspired to set the world's first socialist state on the path of an autocratic, one-party system. This political model was to be imitated all over the eastern half of Europe by the end of the 1940s.

It would be perfectly possible to write a book about the economies of eastern Europe starting from that point, and ignoring pre-war Soviet history. Certainly much of the historical detail is not of great relevance to subsequent developments. But the manner in which the system evolved into its present institutional form *is* worthy of attention, especially since the crucial span of time was actually rather short, from about 1926 to 1930. Before 1926, the regime was first struggling for survival in a bitter Civil War, and then desperately trying to overcome the destructive effects of that war on the economy, whereas by 1930 economic life had acquired its characteristic Stalinist form. The period from 1926 to 1930 was the period of the first experiments in planning; of confrontation with the peasants; of Stalin's rise from a position of first among equals to one of absolute power; and of the development of the highly centralized structure of economic organization now regarded as characteristic of 'Soviet-type economies'.

The choice of such a centralized structure was obviously influenced by the conditions of the time, and in particular by the difficult relationship between the state and the peasantry. The domination of the economy by small independent producers meant that issues of centralization versus decentralization could not be debated purely as questions of socialist economics; they were always overshadowed by the much more explosive question of the struggle between socialist and capitalist economic forms. Moreover the manner in which the government chose to conduct this struggle, displacing free markets by state intervention as rapidly as possible, precipitated difficulties of economic management whose ultimate resolution was to have far-reaching consequences. Not the least significant reason for paying some attention to the Soviet economy in the 1920s is that it helps to shed light on an important contemporary issue: how much the reluctance to carry through far-reaching reforms reflects the enduring legacy of Stalin, and how much it should be seen as a fundamental characteristic of the Soviet type of political system, with or without its Stalinist 'deformations'.

This chapter is divided into three sections. In the first section the situation in the Russian countryside, the Bolshevik interpretation of it and the institutional structure of collective farms as it evolved in the 1930s are discussed. In the second section the evolution of official attitudes to planning and the market, and the role of these attitudes in the developing crisis in agrarian relations in the later 1920s are examined. In the third section the achievements of the industrialization drive of the 1930s are considered in comparison with historical experience up to that date.

Agrarian relations

On the eve of the First World War the economy of the Tsarist empire was no more than partly industrialized. With the help of foreign capital, a considerable industrial sector had developed out of virtually nothing over the previous fifty years, concentrated around St Petersburg and the Baltic States, Moscow and the southern Ukraine. Real income per head was probably not more than half that of France or Germany and a third that of Britain. Nearly half of national income was derived from agriculture, which employed about two-thirds of the population and remained for the most part technically very backward. The urban population accounted for almost 18 per cent of the total. Foodstuffs and agricultural products represented over 70 per cent of exports, whilst finished manufactures accounted for less than 6 per cent (Crisp, 1976; Falkus, 1972).

The abortive revolution of 1905 had revealed that Tsarism was sitting on an agrarian time-bomb. Defeats in the war against Japan had set off disturbances in the towns, which had then spread to the countryside, where peasant seizures of land and burning of manor houses had become frequent in late 1905 and early 1906. The abolition of serfdom in 1861 had done little to improve the lot of the peasants or to alter the structure of agrarian relations, which remained essentially feudal, and many of the provisions of the emancipation legislation inhibited the economic development of the countryside (Gerschenkron, 1965). Population growth had squeezed more and more peasants on to the land, and the expansion of output had barely kept pace. Goldsmith (1961) estimates the growth of agricultural output at 1.7 per cent per annum between 1860 and 1913, whilst annual population growth was 1.5 per cent. In European Russia the average peasant household allotment shrunk from thirty-five acres in 1877 to twenty-eight acres in 1905 (Charques, 1958, p. 63).

After 1905 the government took some steps to accelerate agricultural development, but did nothing to meet peasant demands for the break-up of the large landed estates which covered roughly one-third of the cultivated area. Thus it failed to defuse the agrarian question, and the life of the Provisional Government which took over after the forced abdication of the Tsar in February 1917 was marked by continuous and mounting disorder in the countryside.

Immediately on taking power in October, the Bolsheviks issued a decree expropriating the landowners and handing their estates over to peasant committees for distribution. By this dramatic move, they satisfied the revolutionary feelings of the peasantry, but abandoned for the immediate future a socialist conception of rural life: the peasants chose to chop the estates up into individual allotments of the traditional type. To the peasant, this was historical justice; to the Bolsheviks, it was proof of the incorrigibly petty-bourgeois nature of the peasantry. From that moment on, relations between the government and the peasantry were strained.

It is fair to say that the strains in the relationship were largely of the government's own making. The root of the problem lay with the Bolsheviks' inability to see the Russian countryside as it really was, and their tendency to think of it in terms of some species of Marxist fairy tale. The

Bolsheviks were obsessed by the idea that market forces, left to themselves, would lead to the rapid development of capitalism in the countryside, and that sooner or later (preferably sooner) they would be obliged to precipitate an intensive class conflict between rural capitalists and rural proletarians. This idea created a pervasive allergy to rewarding the economically successful peasant, which conflicted directly with the objective of maximizing the growth rate of agricultural output. The party might have taken, but did not take, the relaxed view that with economic development the agricultural sector would rapidly shrink in importance, so that in the end socialist industry must inevitably prevail over private agriculture, whatever form the latter took (the right wing of the party showed some signs of thinking along these lines – Bukharin spoke at one point of 'riding into socialism on a peasant nag' – but particularly after 1925 the prevailing political atmosphere discouraged the articulation of such ideas).

The hostile external environment probably contributed to this, but only in a minor way. It had long been part of Bolshevik doctrine that after the completion of the radical bourgeois revolution, which would abolish all elements of feudalism, socialism would be built by an alliance of workers and poor peasants against the rural capitalists. Lenin had produced this formulation as early as 1906. From 1917 onwards he made clear on several occasions his desire to organize the poor peasantry as a separate political force. The idea that rich, middle and poor peasantry had distinct and fundamentally conflicting interests was a central component of the political vocabulary of the 1920s. If bitter class struggle in the villages was inevitable, should not the government precipitate it as soon as it felt strong enough to win it?

Yet the reality of village life was that the revolution had promoted a tremendous equalization amongst the peasantry. This may be seen in the results of the statistical surveys of the 1920s. A 1927 sample census showed an average holding of 1 draught animal and 1.1 cows. Amongst the poorest 26 per cent of households, only 20 per cent owned a draught animal and 43 per cent a cow. Amongst the 3.2 per cent of households in the richest category, the average holding was no more than 2.3 draught animals and 2.5 cows. For agricultural implements and machinery the differentiation was somewhat greater: the richest category of households owned five times the average of all means of production, and they farmed 9.4 hectares of cropped ploughland, compared with an average of 4 hectares. But these figures exaggerate the extent of differentiation in two respects. First, they are national figures, so regional differences must account for part of the variation. Secondly, the richer households had more workers (3.42 compared with an average of 2.45) and more family members (7.3 compared with an average of 5.1), so differentiation per person was substantially less than per household. This also helps to explain why only 51 per cent of the richest category of households hired labour and indeed 11 per cent of them sold labour.[1]

In these circumstances it made no sense to interpret every issue of agrarian policy in terms of a titanic struggle between the socialist government and the village capitalists. The rich peasants (kulaks) were working peasants, living in much the same impoverished conditions as their fellows. They did not even begin to represent a separate social class. An anti-kulak policy was therefore inevitably an anti-peasant policy (in the mid-1920s state and co-operative farms covered only about two per cent of the agricultural area, and were not regarded as a commercial success).

From 1926 onwards government policy became increasingly hostile to petty capitalism and therefore to the private peasant. The culmination of this was Stalin's sudden decision to go for all-out collectivization in the autumn of 1929. The background to this decision is discussed in the next section; here its results are briefly summarized. Stalin's move was extremely ill thought out, and born of frustration at the disincentive effects of the government's recent policy. Very little had been decided about the organization of collective farms, and peasants slaughtered livestock on a massive scale to prevent them being collectivized. When the rules were decided some months later, collective farmers were permitted to keep a certain number of animals in private ownership and to graze them on collective pastures, and also to retain some private land around their homes, but none of this was initially clear. Collectivization was accompanied by a punitive policy towards those defined as kulaks, who were not permitted to join the co-operatives.

From an economic point of view the object of collectivization was to bring the peasant within the compass of economic planning, and in particular to remove the peasant's ability to withhold grain from the market (why this was a significant issue will be discussed in the next section). This objective was achieved. The collective farms were subject to compulsory deliveries to the state, for which low prices were paid, and over the years 1929–33 nearly twice as much grain was collected annually from the countryside as in 1928. The low prices meant that the remuneration of collective farmers was also very low, which discouraged effort. Tractors and farm machinery were concentrated in Machine Tractor Stations, for whose services collective farms had to pay in kind. Machine Tractor Stations also had the function of political supervision of the farms in their area.

The policy of depressing peasant consumption did not solve the problem of supplying the towns – food rationing was instituted in 1929 and lasted until 1936 – and acted as a disincentive to effort in agriculture. After a run of mediocre harvests in the early 1930s, there was more slaughtering of farm animals for lack of feed. In 1933 the stock of farm animals was less than half what it had been in 1928, and in many areas peasants themselves died of starvation in 1932–3. After 1933 matters improved, but by the end of the 1930s agricultural output was not very far above its 1929 level, and standards of consumption suffered as a result. In sum, agriculture was the weak point of the economy in the decade after collectivization.

From a formal point of view the collective farm represented a lower degree of socialization than that prevailing elsewhere in the economy, and in Stalin's time in particular was discriminated against on that account. The agricultural equivalent of the socialist industrial enterprise was the state farm, whose workers received wages and were subject to the labour code. Collective farmers' remuneration was in the form of a share of the collective's net income, calculated according to labour days contributed, and was normally paid in kind. Instead of a director, collective farms had a chairman, who was formally elected but in practice appointed by the party. The scope for private production by farm members also distinguished the collective farm from the state enterprise; according to an estimate by Jasny (1949, p. 360), private production accounted for about 25 per cent of collective farm output in 1937.

Planning and the market

Soviet economic policy went through three distinct phases. In the period of the Civil War, from 1918 to early 1921, there were great shortages of everything, and the government budget was hopelessly unbalanced (as indeed it had been since 1915). Rationing was all-pervasive, and many goods were distributed free. Food was requisitioned from the peasantry without payment. Money disappeared from use over a wide sphere of economic activity, and private trade became illegal.

In the spring of 1921 the government proclaimed a 'New Economic Policy' (NEP), which reinstituted market relationships. Peasants received payment for their produce. Private traders and small manufacturing businesses were permitted to function. State enterprises were obliged to run on commercial lines. This retreat was forced by the enormous devastation left by war and mounting evidence that the population would no longer accept the old methods once the threat of counter-revolution had disappeared. In 1921 agricultural output was about 60 per cent of 1913 levels, and factory output was less than a quarter of pre-war figures.

From 1921 to 1925 economic recovery became the overriding goal, and it was not until 1926 that the process was completed.

In 1930 the NEP effectively came to an end, being replaced by a pervasive system of central planning. The major part of agricultural output was now subject to administrative decision: collective farms were given compulsory targets for deliveries of grain and other products to the state. At the same time all other forms of private economic activity were rapidly eliminated, and in 1932 all private trade other than the sale of the peasants' own produce was made illegal (with the exception that collective farms were allowed to sell any surplus output on the free market). This new drive towards socialism took place against the background of the immensely ambitious First Five-Year Plan, adopted in the spring of 1929. The Plan purported to demonstrate the possibility of extremely rapid development. In its 'optimum variant' (which swiftly came to be regarded by the leadership as too pessimistic), it portrayed a doubling of national output in five years, with real wages increasing by 71 per cent and peasant incomes by 30 per cent. This depended on the patently unrealistic hope that labour productivity in industry would increase by 110 per cent and agricultural output by 55 per cent (at the time the Plan was published, it was assumed that collectivization would proceed only slowly, covering only 15 per cent of agricultural production by 1933). The failure to get anywhere near either of these targets was to create enormous inflationary pressure, which was kept under control only by an all-embracing system of rationing.

Thus the First Five-Year Plan inaugurated the period of fully-fledged central planning, characterized by centrally fixed prices and administrative rationing of all investment goods and raw materials. Unlike in the Civil War period, it was not the intention to ration consumer goods. In principle, consumers had free choice over the expenditure of their incomes and their place of employment. For most of the Stalin years, however, there was such extreme shortage of consumer goods, especially food, that rationing was very widespread.

The years of NEP therefore represent the one period of Soviet history when market forces played a significant role in economic life. This happened in the first instance because in early 1921 an incipient revolt against the Civil War system of forced requisitioning of arbitrary quantities of food from peasants made concessions imperative. Requisitioning was replaced by a tax on agricultural output. Private trade and small-scale manufacturing were legalized. State industry had to resume the payment of wages (during the Civil War, workers had simply been issued with rations by the government), and was instructed to operate on commercial lines. The resumption of monetary relations was accompanied by hyperinflation, as the government could not avoid covering its swollen expenditure by printing money. It was only in the spring of 1924, after a currency reform and a programme of budgetary correction, that the price level was stabilized.

There were many signs that the party and the government were not reconciled to NEP as a permanent arrangement. Even in the early 1920s, there was much talk of the differentiation of the peasantry and the rise of the capitalist trader (popularly known as the NEP-man). Up to 1925 these concerns made little impact on policy, because they were overridden by anxiety about economic recovery. Nevertheless they provoked much discussion, and it was taken as axiomatic that the NEP-man should be displaced by state trading organizations as soon as possible. The emotive issue of the rise of the kulak and his domination of the village smouldered continuously in the background. State industry existed in a sea of small private enterprise, so that the role of prices, markets and state intervention could never be debated as a matter of the optimum technique for socialist planning; rather, these issues were always overlain by the much more contentious and politically sensitive one of state/private sector relations. This can be seen in the way that state control very quickly became synonymous with the administrative setting of prices.

The episode known as the 'scissors crisis' is instructive in this regard. The crisis consisted of a yo-yo-like movement in the terms of trade between industry and agriculture (the 'scissors' nomenclature derived from a diagram by Trotsky illustrating the problem). As, in the course of 1921, state subsidies were withdrawn from industry, enterprises competed with one another to sell any asset which they could get their hands on, even setting up stalls in the street to do so. The prices of manufactures began to fall sharply relative to those of agricultural products. In the spring of 1922 the government came to the rescue of industry by virtually eliminating competition, combining the formerly independent trusts into syndicates controlling 70–100 per cent of output of that sector (Carr, 1966, vol. 2, pp. 313–14). This measure was quickly effective, and by August 1922, relative prices were back approximately to their 1913 positions. But in the autumn a good harvest opened the scissors again, and much wider this time, in the opposite direction – so much that by the spring of 1923 there was widespread fear of the political impact on the peasantry. However the government did not choose to reverse its previous decision and to break up the cartels which it had encouraged; instead, it left them in place, restricted industrial credit and set up an apparatus for the state control of industrial prices. At first only wholesale prices were intended to be controlled, since it was reckoned that there were too many independent traders for general control of retail or agricultural prices to be feasible, but these extensions were only a matter of time. 'The doctrine that, even under NEP, price-fixing was a proper and necessary function of government had been clearly established, and was not again contested' (Carr, 1969, p. 149).

The feasibility of price control was always linked with the expansion of state trading organisations, for it was recognized that if private traders dominated the market, effective control of prices would be impossible. This link may be seen in the resolution of May 1924 setting up the People's Commissariat of Internal Trade. This body was directed to regulate all internal trade, *establish firm prices*, and realize effective control over the activity of private capital, with the aim of ensuring the conquest of the market by state and co-operative traders (Carr, 1970, vol. 1, p. 451). In short, the reaction of the party and the government to the scissors crisis demonstrated an overwhelming predisposition towards price fixing by state decree rather than permitting state enterprises to compete freely against one another, a predisposition which was reinforced by the apparently chaotic instability of the terms of trade between agriculture and industry over the years 1921–3.

Price policy was also linked to the whole question of industrialization, which became a prime goal of economic policy once recovery to pre-war output levels had been achieved in 1926. The issue had first been raised by Preobrazhensky, a supporter of the left opposition, in 1923. His argument was that in a society consisting of workers and peasants, a government of the workers would have to extract resources from the peasants to finance industrialization. In the context of the time, given the non-existence of financial institutions in the villages and the low standard of living there, this was taken to mean that industrialization would be financed by taxation more than by borrowing. Preobrazhensky's book was immediately attacked for its alleged failure to recognize the need to maintain the alliance with the peasantry (this was the main charge against the left opposition), but its logic could scarcely be denied once political circumstances were more favourable and the government was less nervous of peasant attitudes. As high rates of industrial growth continued to be achieved in 1926 and 1927, well beyond the recovery period, industrialization schemes became steadily more ambitious, and the peasantry increasingly came to be regarded as an obstacle to these schemes.

The problem was that the government was unwilling to make an explicit statement of its desire to push up the investment rate in industry at the expense of peasant consumption. After the scissors crisis, it became government policy to maintain the terms of trade between agriculture and industry at a more or less fixed rate. The government might have pursued the policy of adding an 'industrialization tax' to the price of manufactured goods, compensating industrial workers for this by a money wage increase, and using the proceeds to finance investment projects. Such a tax would have an upper limit, because peasant (and also workers') consumption would be diverted away from manufactures towards food, so that the market price of food would also rise. Beyond a certain point, the tax would increase food prices as much as the prices of industrial goods, and would then cease to extract resources from the peasants. But there was no evidence that this limit was close to being reached, for it was never tested. Instead the government chose the surreptitious approach of pushing up the rate of investment and imposing highly ambitious cost-cutting targets on industry in an effort to finance the investment out of profits. As the cost-cutting targets were not met, excess demand began to appear in 1927. Since government organizations, aided by discriminatory measures against private traders, had by this time established a dominant position in internal trade, prices remained fixed, and the excess demand expressed itself in shortages. The shortage of manufactured goods was most acute in the villages, which were the most costly markets to supply. This discouraged the peasants from selling their grain, and state purchasing organs found themselves with a shortfall.

It was the reaction of Stalin and his followers to this situation which set the ball rolling towards collectivization. They brought into use a little-known article of the criminal code against speculators, and sent the police into the villages to seek out 'speculative' hoards of grain. Stalin himself led the campaign, spending three weeks in the Urals and Siberia in early 1928. The campaign was successful in its immediate objectives, but obviously had severe disincentive effects on the peasantry. The right was able to force through a 20 per cent increase in grain prices over Stalin's opposition in July 1928, but in the autumn grain procurements again fell well short of target, and in the winter of 1928–9 police methods uncovered much less, probably because there were few large stocks left. Food rationing had to be introduced in the towns.

In 1929 the situation changed in two respects. In April the right opposition was finally defeated and Stalin was left in absolute control; from this moment on his policy was not constrained by any opposing voices of significance within the leadership. The other difference was that collectivization of the peasantry was coming under increasing discussion (although as yet very little had been done about it, and it was assumed that the pace of any collectivization campaign would be slow). But in the autumn of 1929 Stalin, faced with another harvest in which grain procurement was likely to be deficient, suddenly decided to take a big gamble that the whole problem of the recalcitrant peasant could be solved once and for all by immediate collectivization. Once collectivized, the peasant would be deprived of the ability to withhold grain from the state, and the industrialization campaign would be established on a much more secure basis. Collectives could be subjected to mandatory supply quotas, so that state needs would have priority and the peasant would receive the residual – a dramatic reversal of the existing situation. The effects of this decision on agricultural output have already been discussed. It created such a shortage of food, as well as of urban housing and of other consumer goods, that the industrialization programme could really only be pushed forward on the basis of terror and police methods. The entire power of the state apparatus was required to force the population to accept the sacrifices involved. In effect, the atmosphere and methods were those of a war economy, with the ruthless pursuit of state-determined priorities and severe reductions in living standards, and it is not surprising that an extreme concentration of decision-making at the centre was used to achieve this. Throughout the 1930s, the planning process had a distinct resemblance to the conduct of a military operation: published plans meant little, and the planners were constantly having to issue new instructions as new problems appeared.

It is clear that the events of this period bear the mark of Stalin's impetuous, brutal style. Who else would have handled the peasant question in this manner? But the seeds of his solution lie much deeper, in the attitudes pervading the Communist Party throughout the 1920s. There was a well-established belief that socialism meant fixed prices. The rapid relative price changes of the early 1920s seemed decisive proof of the chaotic nature of the free market. Pursuing this line of thought, the government elected, as early as 1924, to use price control as part of its struggle with the private sector. In doing so, it put itself in the uncomfortable position of having to take public responsibility for price movements. This created considerable reluctance to move them at all. There was equal reluctance to establish a focus for peasant discontent by explicitly shifting the terms of trade against agriculture. It was more tempting to push up the rate of investment regardless, making optimistic assumptions about industrial profits, and to blame industry for failing to meet its targets when the resulting excess demand created shortages. Without administrative control of prices, inflation would have resulted. Since inflation was suppressed, its political impact was muted and in practice ignored. What was not appreciated was that the shortages would reduce peasant sales of grain as surely as an increase in industrial prices. In an environment of anxiety about and intense hostility to the rise of the kulak, it was easy to regard this peasant behaviour as evidence of kulak speculation, rather than as the rational response of small producers to the situation on the market. Thus the peasant was transformed by price control into the enemy of the state, and the rapid socialization of agriculture was the almost inevitable response.

Economic growth in the 1930s

Marxists had always tended to believe that under socialism the economy would develop faster than under capitalism. Stalin himself proclaimed the objective of catching up with the capitalist countries as fast as possible, and portrayed it as a question of national survival. How, then, does the Soviet growth record in the 1930s compare with that of more advanced countries at a similar stage of development?

I shall be concerned essentially with the period 1929 to 1937, covered by the first two five-year plans, since the third, which started in 1938, was interrupted by the outbreak of war. The official Soviet figures show that plan targets for industrial production as a whole were met for both the First and Second Five-Year Plans, but only because underfulfilment of consumer goods targets was offset by overfulfilment of producer goods plans. The official figures for the First Five-Year Plan show an enormous shortfall in agriculture (58 per cent of planned output achieved) and for real wages and labour productivity (both 65 per cent of plan), combined with considerable overfulfilment in the undesirable areas of industrial employment (174 per cent of plan) and the average money wage (144 per cent). For the Second Five-Year Plan (1933–7), the official figures estimate that industrial labour productivity and real wages grew as planned, but agricultural output reached only 63 per cent of plan (77 per cent if 1926/7 prices are used) (Zaleski, 1962, Table 58; 1980, Table 129).

Such estimates indicate a relatively poor performance for consumption, agriculture and labour productivity, but tremendous achievements in the realm of investment goods. Unfortunately independent estimates of plan fulfilment are not nearly so favourable, particularly for industrial production. The 1926/7 prices which are used in official estimates rapidly became out of date, and present an abnormally favourable picture because the fastest-growing sectors had particularly high prices at that time. Subsequently, their relative price fell, so that calculations using a later year as a base result in significantly lower growth rates. Further factors tending to inflate the official index are the introduction of new products at prices based on their high initial costs of production, and the use of gross outputs, so that outputs which act as inputs are counted twice. This latter procedure inflates the total, but does not affect the growth rate unless there are changes in institutional structure affecting statistical reporting. In the 1930s trusts and syndicates were gradually eliminated, leaving the industrial commissariat (termed 'ministry' from 1946) as the only tier of industrial administration between the central planners and the enterprise. Enterprises then replaced trusts as the basic statistical unit, which may have caused some intra-trust transactions to appear as additional gross output. Western estimates have tried to correct for this effect.

According to the official Soviet index, industrial production grew at an average annual rate of 16.8 per cent from 1928 to 1940, and of 18.1 per cent from 1928 to 1937. Western estimates for 1928 to 1940 range from a low of 8.4 per cent to a high of 13.6 per cent per annum, all with a marked slowdown after 1937 (Nutter, 1962, Tables 32, 33). This is still fast, but a long way short of the official figure. For agriculture, the discrepancies are much smaller. All authorities agree that output fell by about 20 per cent from 1928 to 1932, and had recovered by the later 1930s to slightly above its 1928 level. In the exceptionally favourable year 1937, agricultural output was less than 10 per cent above 1928, so the growth rate of this sector averaged less than 1 per cent per annum.

How did real wages fare in the 1930s, according to unofficial estimates? Calculations are difficult for the period 1929–35, because of the prevalence of rationing and shortages, and the consequent absence of a satisfactory price index. It is certain, however, that real wages fell from 1928 up until 1934, and then began to recover quite fast. By 1937 they were nevertheless still rather less than in 1928. According to the estimates of Janet Chapman (1963), real wages fell by 15 per cent if the cost of living is measured at 1937 prices, and 42 per cent if it is measured at 1928 prices, and were even lower by 1940. A Soviet historian of prices likewise concludes that there was a significant fall from 1928 to 1937.[2] In view of the pitiful rates of pay on collective farms, it is also difficult to believe that peasant incomes were higher in 1937 than in 1928, despite the fact that 1937 was a year of an exceptionally good harvest. Measured by *per capita* consumption, however, the fall in living standards was almost negligible, and when communal services such as education and health are included, a 10 per cent increase is registered, though the considerable expansion in education is perhaps better regarded as investment in human skills. This discrepancy reflects the improvement in living standards of new entrants to the labour force (Chapman, 1963, Table VI.1).

The general picture, then, is one of fast industrial growth with stagnant agriculture and consumption, all against a background of mass terror and ideological bludgeoning. There is no doubt of the enormity of the human cost, but how does the growth rate compare with that of other

Table 1.1 Average growth rates of output and labour input in USSR industry (per cent per annum)

Period	*Output measured at:* 1928 prices	1937 prices	1950 prices	Man-hours of labour input
1928–32	18.1	7.1	7.1	10.1
1932–7	17.7	12.6	10.9	4.2
1937–40	10.8	8.8	6.1	6.0

Source: R. Powell, in A. Bergson and S. Kuznets (eds), *Economic Trends in the Soviet Union*, Cambridge, Mass.: Harvard University Press, 1963, tables IV.1 and IV.3

countries up until that time? As Abram Bergson and others have shown, the measured growth rate of the economy depends greatly on whether 1928 or 1937 expenditure weights are used. The almost stagnant agricultural sector suffered the greatest increase in prices between these two dates, and the service sector the smallest. A calculation using 1937 weights therefore shows a slower growth rate than one using 1928 weights. But the problem also makes a great deal of difference within the industrial sector, as table 1.1 shows. There is little agreement between the different estimates except on the deceleration of industry after 1937. We may accept that 1928 weights were out of date for the Second Five-Year Plan period, but they may be a better reflection of true opportunity costs than 1937 weights for the First Five-Year Plan.

Whatever the exact figures, an average growth rate of industrial production of 10 per cent or more per annum sustained over a twelve-year period is a formidable achievement, for which there was certainly little precedent at the time. The United States grew faster in the period 1870–1913 than any European country (Maddison, 1969, p. 31), but its manufacturing production, in its fastest decade of growth from 1900 to 1910, grew at an average rate of only 5.6 per cent per annum. One has to turn to later experience, such as Japan from 1955 to 1973, to find manufacturing growth rates to match those of the USSR in the 1930s.

Was the USSR's industrial growth achieved by means of very fast expansion of industrial employment or by rapid productivity growth? Table 1.1 shows labour input increasing at 10.1 per cent per annum in 1928–32, 4.2 per cent per annum in 1932–7 and 6 per cent per annum in 1937–40. This suggests very rapid productivity growth from 1932 to 1937, rather less between 1937 and 1940, and either very rapid or negative productivity growth from 1928 to 1932, depending on which output series is used. Table 1.2 illustrates the results of an alternative calculation by Warren Nutter. The figures for output tend to be lower,

Table 1.2 Alternative estimates of industrial growth rates in the USSR (per cent per annum)

		Growth rates of:	
Period	*Total industrial output*	*Man-hours*	*Output per man-hour*
1928–33	8.4	7.2	1.2
1933–7	16.7	9.5	6.5
1937–40	3.8	10.4	−5.8

Source: Nutter (1962), Tables 30, 39, 40

and for labour input higher, than Powell's, but once again the Second Five-Year Plan period emerges with the highest rates of productivity growth (the massive intake of untrained labour in the First Five-Year Plan probably held back productivity growth). In comparison with the USA, these figures are once again quite impressive. Although output per unit of labour input increased 5.6 per cent per annum in US manufacturing from 1919 to 1929, this was exceptional: in no other decade before 1948 did it exceed 2 per cent per annum (Kendrick, 1961, Table 40).

For GNP, we expect slower growth rates because of the inclusion of the virtually stagnant agricultural sector. Bergson has calculated the growth rate of GNP over the 1928–37 period as 5.5 per cent per annum if measured at 1937 rouble factor cost, and as 11.9 per cent if measured at 1928 rouble factor cost.[3] The latter figure is certainly too high, because the 1928 price structure rapidly became obsolete, but even the lower figure comfortably exceeds the US average of 4.3 per cent per annum from 1870 to 1913. Moreover a comparison of GNP per capita is even more favourable to the USSR: no western country exceeded a growth rate of GNP per capita of 2.2 per cent per annum in the period 1870 to 1913. In the USSR, population grew at an annual rate of about 1 per cent between the census years of 1929 and 1939, so real GNP per capita grew by at least 4.5 per cent per annum during the 1930s. Moreover, unlike in later periods, this growth was not accompanied by a marked rise in the capital-output ratio; Moorsteen and Powell (1966, Table T53) estimate that this ratio only rose from 1.68 in 1928 to 1.73 in 1937.

What proportion of its resources did the USSR have to devote to investment in order to achieve this? According to Moorsteen and Powell (1966, Table T50), gross fixed investment represented 20.3 per cent of GNP in 1928 and 21.1 per cent in 1937, but then fell rapidly to under 13 per cent by 1940. These figures are calculated at current prices. Measured at constant prices (either 1928 or 1937) the investment ratio rose

Table 1.3 Shares of the GNP of the USSR at factor cost (per cent)

	1928	*1937*
Private consumption	64.7	52.5
Communal services	5.1	10.5
Government administration	2.7	3.2
Defence	2.5	7.9
Gross fixed investment	22.5	21.9
Investment in stocks	2.4	3.9
Total	100.0	100.0

Source: Bergson (1961), Tables 23 and 33

rapidly during this period, as the relative price of equipment fell very fast. If we assume that the fall in the relative price of machinery was a reasonably accurate reflection of the reduction in its opportunity cost as industrialization proceeded (and not just a failure to raise its prices in line with consumer prices), then the current price calculation is more relevant.

Table 1.3 gives shares of GNP at current prices in 1928 and 1937 according to Bergson's calculations. The investment ratio is similar to that calculated by Moorsteen and Powell. What the table shows is the tremendous squeeze on private consumption in the 1930s, to the advantage of communal services and defence. The investment ratio remained more or less constant, and did not markedly exceed that of the United States or Germany at a similar stage of development (Lewis, 1978, p. 71), but the squeeze on private consumption was exceptional. It enabled the authorities to combine a high rate of investment with heavy expenditures on defence and education, instead of having to make a choice between them. When full allowance is made for the punishments meted out to kulaks and others and the general brutalization of life under the terror, this was forced industrialization at enormous cost to the current generation.

Nevertheless the impression left by this experience was that catching up with the most advanced countries within a few decades was a feasible goal for socialist economies. Many Communists in eastern Europe enthusiastically adopted Soviet-style plans in the early 1950s, in the belief that they would rapidly overcome their countries' backwardness. In 1961, Khrushchev rashly wrote into the Soviet party programme the goal of catching up with the United States by 1980. As we shall see in chapter 7, this optimism was proved wrong not so much in expecting fast growth under socialism as in failing to anticipate that the rest of Europe would be able to accelerate its growth rate after 1945.

Notes

1 Jasny (1949) reproduces relevant tables from this sample (pp. 780–3) and discusses the results at some length (pp. 163–82). On the basis of one table showing that better-off households have more adult male workers, Jasny claims (pp. 165–6) that adult male workers are of particular significance to household income. However this appears to be an incorrect deduction: better-off households have more adult males because they have more persons in general – the *proportion of* adult males varies very little with income.

2 Malafayev (1964, Table 21). With 1928 = 100, Malafayev gives money wages in 1937 at 482 and retail prices at 536, implying a fall in real wages of about 10 per cent. He uses the official index of prices for state and co-operative trade in these calculations. This is not unreasonable since free market prices were little different from state prices in 1937, unlike a few years earlier, but it excludes service sector prices, which rose rather less than this. Chapman's money wage index for 1937 is only 405; the discrepancy arises because Malafayev uses a 1928 figure which includes unemployed workers (see Note 1 to his Table 21). For 1940, Malafayev's figures put real wages back at the 1928 level, a rise of 12 per cent since 1937. However by 1940 serious shortages had reappeared, and free market prices had once again raced ahead of state prices. Janet Chapman's calculations take account to this, whereas Malafayev's do not.

3 Bergson (1961, Table 52). The alternative calculation by Moorsteen and Powell (1966) yields 6.2 per cent and 11.9 per cent respectively.

2

The USSR and Eastern Europe since 1945

Introduction

This chapter provides a brief survey of developments in the USSR and eastern Europe since 1945, as a background to the more theoretical discussion of economic behaviour under central planning in chapters 3 and 4. Some reference is made to the economic reforms of the 1960s, but these are treated in more detail in later chapters. The second half of the chapter concentrates on trends and cycles in output, using official figures for net material product. Though the accuracy and reliability of official figures have been questioned by western observers (this issue is discussed further in chapter 7), few would argue that they fail to capture the broad pattern of economic growth. A final section surveys the major developments in the agricultural sector, whose institutional structure remains significantly different from that of industry.

From 1945 to the death of Stalin

For the USSR the Second World War was immensely destructive. The number of dead may well have reached 20 million. A large part of Soviet territory was occupied and denuded of useful assets, and the bulk of the hostilities took place on Soviet soil, along a vast front that stretched from the Baltic to the Black Sea. In 1941 the Germans reached the outskirts of Leningrad and Moscow. In 1942 they advanced in the south, towards the oilfields around the Caspian, and their progress was only finally reversed in the battle of Stalingrad in January 1943.

During the war the output of the areas not under German control steadily increased, but the destruction in the occupied areas was such that national income in 1945 was probably about 20 per cent below its 1940 level (Moorsteen and Powell, 1966, Table T47). There was an immense task of reconstruction to be carried out. Stalin emerged as a war leader with enhanced prestige and power, despite the fact that he was personally largely responsible for the military unpreparedness of the country in June 1941, having ignored intelligence warnings of the impending attack, and that he had been in a state of nervous collapse for a week after the invasion. He soon made it clear that after the war the patterns of the 1930s would be resumed. In politics, the terror, which had been suspended during the emergency conditions of wartime, began again. Many prisoners of war returning from Germany were incarcerated on arriving home, on suspicion that they had surrendered unnecessarily. In 1949 Nikolai Voznesensky, the head of Gosplan, was arrested and shot. The secret police, at once the instrument and the stimulant of Stalin's paranoia, had unlimited powers and ran a vast economic empire of labour camps. In a tragic and absurd episode in 1952, a mostly Jewish group of Kremlin doctors was accused of having attempted to poison a number of political leaders over a period of several years. They were saved by the dictator's death on 5 March 1953, and rehabilitated; one, however, had committed suicide in prison. In intellectual life, any expression of independent ideas ran the risk of condemnation for right-wing or Trotskyite deviation and sabotage (and often both), and idiotic scientific ideas, such as those of Trofim Lysenko, were taken up officially because they pandered to the wishful thinking of Stalin and his cronies.

In economics, the emphasis was once again on heavy industry and high rates of investment. This resulted in an impressive growth rate, but a delayed recovery of consumption. By 1948 GNP had returned to its 1940 level, and by 1950 it was 21 per cent above it (Moorsteen and Powell, 1966). But when prices were increased in December 1947 to soak up the excess demand built up during the war, enabling real wages to be accurately measured, they proved to be still far below 1940 levels, and may well have been not much less than half the pre-war figure. However, from 1948 to 1953 retail prices were cut and money wages increased in every year. According to Chapman's estimates (1963, pp. 166–71) real wages more than doubled between 1948 and 1954, by which time they were perhaps 15 per cent above the 1928 level. Until Stalin's death peasant living standards remained depressed by low procurement prices for agricultural products, and had probably experienced no increase at all relative to 1928. Despite this, consumption per capita in the USSR in 1954 was nearly twice what it had been in 1928. This was the effect of the elimination of unemployment, a fall in the number of dependants per worker (many more women were in paid employment), a shift of population from rural to better remunerated urban occupations, and an expansion in the number of higher-paid jobs. Life was bleak in Stalin's last

Table 2.1 Investment and capital-output ratios in the USSR 1936–60

	Average proportion of GNP (%)	
Period	*Gross fixed investment*	*Net capital stock*
1936–40	17.2	1.82
1946–50	20.0	1.94[a]
1951–5	22.3	1.94
1956–60	28.8	2.11

[a] 1.87 for 1948–50. The higher figures for 1946 and 1947 reflect wartime disruption of output.
Source: Moorsteen and Powell (1966), Tables T50 and T53

years, but the population was beginning to experience some of the fruits of industrialization.

The death of Stalin was soon followed by indications that things were going to be somewhat different in future. Political prisoners began to be released. A 'new course' was proclaimed, the essence of which was considerable concessions to consumers. Beria, Stalin's last secret police chief, was arrested in June 1953 and later shot on the pretext that he was plotting to establish personal power for himself; measures were taken to curb the power of the secret police. Stalin himself was not yet attacked, and continued to be quoted as the great authority, until Khrushchev's secret speech denouncing him at the Twentieth CPSU Congress in February 1956.

Retail prices were cut on average by 10 per cent on 1 April 1953, whilst procurement prices for agricultural products were raised substantially, so that on average in 1956 they were 2.5 times what they had been in 1952 (Malafayev, 1964, p. 412); at the same time, a more lenient policy was pursued towards private plots. For the first time since collectivization, significant material concessions were being made to the peasant. In October 1953 higher plans for consumption goods output were announced. These policies were associated particularly with Malenkov, the chairman of the Council of Ministers. But they were not to last. In February 1955 Malenkov was forced to resign, ostensibly for failing to give the proper priority to heavy industry. Thereafter the propensity of the system towards high rates of investment reasserted itself, as table 2.1 illustrates. The figures show a clear tendency in the post-war period towards an ever higher investment ratio, and a fall in capital productivity. Neither of these tendencies died with Stalin; indeed, as we shall see later, they have been a significant feature of Soviet bloc economies for some time.

Table 2.2 The economic development of eastern Europe in 1945

Country	*Percentage of labour force in agriculture*	*Net national product per capita in 1938 ($)*	*Population (millions)*
Bulgaria	26	176	15.2
Czechoslovakia	65	104	34.5
Hungary	51	112	8.9
Poland	80	70–75	19.2
Romania	80	68	6.2
Yugoslavia	76	81	15.0

Sources: Spulber (1957), Tables 1 and 2; M. Kaser, *The Economic Development of Eastern Europe 1919–1975* Vol. 1, Oxford: Clarendon Press, 1985, p. 532

In eastern Europe the situation on the ground left the USSR in a decisive position to influence events in all countries north of Yugoslavia and Greece, because of the presence of Soviet forces; in addition, the informal agreement at Yalta assigned these countries to the Soviet sphere of influence. At the very least, the Soviet Union was interested in ensuring friendly governments in these countries, since only one of them (Czechoslovakia) had resisted the temptation to nibble off bits of Soviet territory in the past: Poland had declared war in 1920, and Hungary, Romania and Bulgaria had allied themselves with the Axis powers in 1941.

Considerable territorial changes and population movements occurred in 1945. The Soviet Union gained the Baltic republics, a slice of Prussia, half the pre-war territory of Poland (mostly what the USSR had had to concede in 1920), and the eastern tip of Slovakia and Moldavia. Poland was compensated by expansion in the west. The German population was expelled from the territories ceded in the east, and from Czechoslovakia (where it numbered 2½ million) and Hungary.

Economically, there was a clear gradation in the region from northwest to southeast. The Czech lands and the Soviet zone of Germany (which became the German Democratic Republic in 1949) were industrialized areas, broadly on a par with western Europe. Hungary and Poland had some industry, although not a great deal, but the area from eastern Poland and Slovakia down to Romania, Bulgaria and Yugoslavia was almost entirely agricultural. This is illustrated in the figures presented in table 2.2.

The political strategy of Communist parties in these countries in 1945 was to continue the anti-fascist alliance but to manoeuvre it in an anti-capitalist direction. Coalition governments were formed, and the states

were described as people's democracies. These governments carried out considerable nationalization, and enacted land reforms breaking up large properties and distributing them to peasants on the lines of 1917, but the economies retained a sizeable private sector and did not introduce Soviet-type planning. The governments of these countries behaved very differently from the Yugoslavs, who were not constrained by the presence of other political parties and moved swiftly to imitate the Soviet model in all respects, until their dispute with Stalin in 1948 began to make them embarrassed about it. In Romania, the king was not forced to abdicate until 1947.

Undoubtedly this restraint suited Stalin initially, for he did not wish to antagonize his allies openly. But as relations with the United States deteriorated and the Cold War reached its height, it began to seem imperative to attach the east European states firmly to the socialist camp, and not to allow scope for any sort of western intervention there. Accordingly, from the end of 1947, the east European countries were shifted swiftly over to the Soviet model, which many Communists were in any case yearning to imitate. Those leaders who attempted to resist this were removed or marginalized. In Poland, Gomułka was replaced as Party Secretary by Bierut; suspected or alleged Titoists were discovered throughout eastern Europe. Non-communist parties either accepted a completely subordinate role or were banned. In many countries (though not Poland or the GDR) there were Soviet-type show trials, with public confessions followed by execution; the most prominent victims were Rajk, Foreign Minister of Hungary, in 1949, and Slansky, a leader of the Czech Communist Party, in 1952. Industry was effectively 100 per cent nationalized, and even in the service sector private enterprise was drastically curtailed (Brus, 1986, Table 23.1; the process had not yet gone as far in the GDR, because of uncertainty about the future of Germany). In the countryside collectivization campaigns began, and Soviet-style medium-term plans were devised to run to 1955, emphasizing investment in heavy industry.

In agriculture, discriminatory measures of all kinds were used to eliminate the kulaks and encourage the peasants to join co-operatives, though, as in the USSR, the results in terms of output tended to be disappointing. The pace of this campaign varied widely: by 1953 the socialist sector (state and collective farms) embraced 63 per cent of arable land in Bulgaria, 43 per cent in Czechoslovakia and 40 per cent in Hungary, but only 25 per cent in Romania and 19 per cent in Poland (Spulber, 1957, Table 66). For all countries the development plans envisaged a faster rate of growth of output of producers' than of consumer goods. Each country built its own steel mills and engineering

factories; reliance on international trade and specialization was to all intents and purposes nil. Cut off from western markets by a political blockade, each country's plan was a replica of the autarkic Soviet model, with the same consequences: depression of real wages, shortages of consumer goods and long delays in the completion of projects. From 1950 to 1952, the investment ratio increased rapidly, and real wages fell significantly, after a steady expansion during the years 1947–9.

The death of Stalin and the proclamation of the 'new course' in the USSR stimulated similar developments in the east European countries. Official statements about fulfilling the five-year plan in four years, which had been frequent in 1952, gave way to proclamations of a period of consolidation, with a deceleration of investment and greater attention to consumer needs. The collectivization programme was virtually halted. In the GDR in June 1953, the reluctance of the leadership to embark on such a new course, and in particular to rescind a proposed 10 per cent increase in work norms without adjustment of pay, set off a series of strikes which forced the government to back down. However, the consumerist interlude lasted only as long as Malenkov remained in power in the USSR. By the time he fell, his line was being condemned as a right-wing deviation all over eastern Europe, as in the USSR, and economic planning fell back into its old pattern.

In the Stalin period there was a clear net transfer of resources from eastern Europe to the USSR. First of all, ex-enemy countries had to pay substantial reparations over a period of six years (later extended to eight), mostly to the USSR. This was a great burden on the economies of the GDR, Hungary and Romania (Bulgaria had to pay smaller reparations to Greece and Yugoslavia). In the Soviet zone of Germany much equipment was dismantled and shipped off to the Soviet Union. The sizeable German assets in the ex-enemy countries also accrued to the USSR, and formed its contribution to the joint Soviet-Hungarian, Soviet-Romanian and Soviet-Bulgarian enterprises in these countries. Such joint companies also existed in the GDR. These companies had Soviet managers, enjoyed virtually complete tax exemption, and were often able to use their contacts with each other to corner markets. Half of all the profits of these companies accrued to the USSR. In addition, it would seem that Romania continued to make free deliveries of oil to the USSR for some time after it had fulfilled its reparations obligations, and it was admitted in 1956 that deliveries of cheap Polish coal, originally in return for German machinery dismantled by the USSR, had continued longer than was justified. In sum, Stalin made use of many devices to extract resources from the east Europeans, treating them as fodder to the greater glory of the USSR just as if they were Russian peasants.

After his death, however, the new Soviet leaders fairly quickly recognized that such an obviously exploitative relationship with eastern Europe was impolitic, and in 1954 most of the joint companies were liquidated and their assets nationalized. Although the USSR initially required some financial compensation for this, payment being spread over a period of years, it in fact waived all such claims after the Hungarian upheaval of 1956. Since 1956, considerable efforts have been made to avoid any suspicion of exploitation in trading relationships. Where possible inter-socialist trade has utilized world market prices of the recent past. Indeed if one takes into account the delayed adjustment of the price of east European oil imports from the Soviet Union after 1973 and the subsidies which have been paid to east European governments in political difficulties, the flow of resources has been the reverse of what it was before 1956 (Holzman, 1986).

De-Stalinization and after

This section summarizes political and economic developments over the last three decades. Various aspects of economic performance will be discussed in detail in the remaining sections of this chapter, and in chapters 3, 4 and 7.

By 1955 Khrushchev was clearly emerging as the key figure in the Soviet leadership. It was he who led the delegation to Belgrade to mend fences with Tito, and it was he who, in February 1956, made the famous speech denouncing Stalin to a closed session of the Twentieth CPSU Congress. In economic matters, he differed from Stalin most notably in his willingness to recognize that agriculture was being held back by the disincentive effect of Stalin's tribute policy. In the 1950s, the rural population at last began to share in the increased prosperity of the country. But in other respects, Khrushchev's economic ideas were rather traditional. He got carried away by grand schemes, such as the Virgin Lands campaign, a plan to cultivate millions of hectares of marginal steppe land at a hectic pace; he pushed through a fundamental administrative reorganization of the planning system, replacing industrial ministries by regional bodies as the intermediaries between the central planners and the enterprise; and he remained obsessed by catching up with the capitalist countries, writing into the 1961 party programme the goal of overtaking the USA by 1980. But it was not until 1962 that any article advocating reform of the planning *mechanism* was to appear in *Pravda*, even though such questions had been discussed in specialist journals for many years. Khrushchev was an energetic leader, but his solutions to problems were often misconceived and over-ambitious, which eventually caused his colleagues to overthrow him in October 1964.

In industry, as already mentioned, Khrushchev continued to pursue a high growth rate policy. In 1958 he introduced a new seven-year plan, to run from 1959 to 1965, to supersede the Sixth Five-Year Plan running from 1956 to 1960. In the seven-year plan producers' goods output was planned to grow substantially faster than that of consumer goods. But the most dramatic move was the decision in 1957 to go over from an industrial to a regional planning basis. Instead of industrial ministries, 105 regional economic councils (*sovnarkhozy*) were to supervise the enterprises of their region. This reform was intended as a cure for the tendency of ministries to put their own interests before those of the country as a whole. As might have been predicted, however, 'ministerialism' was simply replaced by 'regionalism', which was even more dangerous in that it was liable to have a political component (particularly as in eleven cases an economic region was coextensive with a republic). It also prevented the authorities from effectively supervising particular industries and their technical problems. One of the first acts of Khrushchev's successors after his removal was to reverse this reform.[1]

Khrushchev took a particular interest in agricultural development. In 1954 he promoted a campaign to sow grain on millions of hectares of virgin steppe in the drier regions, where the unreliability of rainfall had hitherto inhibited cultivation. The first year's good results caused this effort, known as the Virgin Lands campaign, to be considerably expanded. Up to 1958 this campaign met with brilliant success. According to the official figures, the grain harvest was increased by more than 20 per cent in five years. Then trouble began. For the next five years, agricultural output stagnated. The soil of the Virgin Lands was quickly exhausted and suffered from wind erosion, and livestock numbers failed to increase as planned because of unfavourable price changes in 1958, when policy also became more punitive towards the private plot. In the same year the government had abolished the Machine Tractor Stations, and ordered that their equipment should be sold to the collective farms, which often lacked the knowledge to operate it properly. Other innovations of Khrushchev's were less significant, but he continued to indulge his mania for reorganizations, and in 1962 even split the Communist Party into industrial and agricultural sections.

With Khrushchev's removal in October 1964, there was a further reassertion of the principle of collective leadership, and it was some years before Leonid Brezhnev became the obviously dominant figure. Khrushchev's successors were anxious to create an atmosphere of stability. They did not want a return to Stalinism, nor did they want vigorous de-

Stalinization and raking over the past. Above all they wanted a stable system of administration after Khrushchev's upheavals. In the economic sphere, living standards increased steadily, and Soviet households began to possess a reasonable stock of consumer durables. The leaders experimented with decentralizing economic reforms, but within the traditional framework of central planning, and gradually abandoned them when they ceased to produce the anticipated results (these reforms will be considered in more detail in chapter 3). They invested considerable resources in defence, in an effort to achieve military parity with the US, and the cost of this policy probably contributed to the poor performance of the economy. They presided over a noticeable deceleration of economic growth, without giving any indication that they had much idea what to do about it. By the 1980s so little progress had been made in catching up with the US that the goal had to be dropped altogether from the party programme. The leadership remained extremely stable, and by the 1970s had aged so much that the USSR stood out as a gerontocracy. A certain Brezhnev personality cult even began to develop, thereby brilliantly confirming Marx's dictum that 'history always repeats itself, the first time as tragedy, the second time as farce'. Even when Brezhnev was so ill that he could scarcely function, he retained all his posts and his condition was hidden from the public.

The most troublesome sector of the economy in the Brezhnev period was agriculture. In the period 1965–70, agricultural output increased considerably, as a result of a combination of favourable weather, a more relaxed policy towards the private plot and improved incentives for livestock production. In an effort to raise the output of meat and dairy products, investment in agriculture was steadily increased. Nevertheless, in 1971 the USSR, a traditional grain exporter, began to import significant quantities of grain. In 1981–5, harvests were so far below target that no figures were published until 1986. When they were published, the extent of the failure of agricultural policy was clear, as table 2.3 shows. The grain harvest, still the crucial element of agricultural production, fell short of plan targets by over 20 per cent.

Thus the Brezhnev years were indeed stable, but in many respects increasingly unsatisfactory. Since Brezhnev's death political life has taken a dramatic turn. His immediate successor, Yuri Andropov, launched a drive against corruption, but died within a year. He was succeeded by the elderly Konstantin Chernenko, widely regarded as a Brezhnev man who would put the brake on this campaign, but he too died shortly after taking office. Then the leadership passed to the relatively youthful Mikhail Gorbachev, who has initiated a massive campaign for change and attacked the party style of the Brezhnev era in the

Table 2.3 The Soviet agricultural sector 1951–85

Period	*Grain harvest (million tons)*	*Share of agriculture in total investment (%)*
1951–60	105.0	16.0
1961–5	130.3	16.2
1966–70	167.6	17.0
1971–5	181.6	19.9
1976–80	205.0	20.4
1981–5	180.3	19.2*

* 1981–4

Sources: Clarke and Matko (1983), p. 147
The Guardian 19 November 1986
UNECE (1968), p. 151; (1976), Part II, p. 100; (1985/6), p. 177

most scathing terms. Gorbachev's behaviour can only be explained as a response to a perception that the CPSU has drifted into a state of crisis. Under Brezhnev its simplistic propaganda had lost credibility with a highly educated society, which increasingly relapsed into cynicism, moral scepticism and a fascination with western consumer products. Gorbachev's programme is a complex mixture of old and new remedies. It is conservative in the sense that it seeks to preserve the existing parameters of power, but radical in its search for a new relationship between party and people. Without amending the one-party state or the framework of central planning, he is seeking a new openness in the media and the state, in order to close the 'credibility gap'. This has created a fascinating situation, because for the first time the party's arrogance in relation to the community is being highlighted for criticism. Gorbachev has repeatedly attacked 'those officials who are accustomed to wielding power without being accountable to the people' and insisted that 'democracy is order of a high level, based not on unquestioning obedience and blind performance of the tasks set, but based on the participation of people in society's affairs, with full rights and initiative' (speech to the Congress of Soviet Trade Unions, as reported in *The Guardian* 26 February 1987). This is fine stuff, but a little perplexing in a Soviet context. If taken seriously, it would give the people considerable power to criticize the party, without being able to replace it with another. The situation would encourage sniping and negative criticism. In the long run, its effect could well be to undermine the authority of the party, without offering it any new source of legitimacy. For this reason, the average party official is likely to view accountability in an increasingly negative light. It is possible that, although Gorbachev's programme is a reaction to a crisis of legitimacy of the party, its long-run effect could be to deepen that crisis by discrediting the authoritarian patterns of behaviour which are natural to a one-party system.

In economic matters, Gorbachev has given a new impetus to discussion of reform, although the ideas he has so far espoused, such as emphasis on contract fulfilment and self-financing by ministries and enterprises, are not new, and have been part of the official programme since at least 1979. By 1987 it was clear that there was a struggle going on about precisely how far such principles were to be taken, and some new experiments began in 1988. On the record of previous episodes of reform, there must be considerable doubt about whether Soviet economic performance can be greatly improved, or whether growth in living standards will continue to bump along at a rate close to the politically acceptable minimum, as many observers expect (Bergson and Levine, 1983).

In eastern Europe, the period since 1953 has witnessed economic trends similar to the USSR: deceleration of growth, inefficiency of investment and difficulties with technical progress. Politically, the trend has been towards increasing independence: policy in these countries no longer copies that of the USSR in the same immediate way that it did before 1956. This was only natural once the heretical Yugoslavs had been welcomed back into the fold. Still, it might have been a slower process than it was, because the USSR had many ways of applying pressure in the other east European countries which were not available in more distant Yugoslavia (or Albania).

The initial impetus for change came from the events of 1956 in Poland and Hungary. In both those countries, after the contents of Khrushchev's secret speech became known, there was considerable oppositional activity. The Stalinist leader in Poland, Bierut, had died in March. In June workers in Poznań staged a demonstration which initially focused on economic demands, but became increasingly political and ended with an attack on several public buildings, including the town's police headquarters. The next day the rebellion was suppressed with the help of tanks, and 54 people died in the action. This set off a political crisis which led first to the rehabilitation and then, in October, to re-election to the leadership of Gomułka, who had been Prime Minister from 1945 to 1948, but was under arrest during the Stalinist period. Gomułka made a number of concessions to the popular movement, increasing real wages and experimenting with economic reforms; his most spectacular move, and the only one of permanent significance as it turned out, was the dismantling of collective farms.

In Hungary, a similar movement led to the replacement of the Stalinist

Rakosi by another Stalinist, Gerö, in July 1956. This scarcely satisfied popular demands, and in October the Polish events stimulated even greater opposition activity; Gerö was replaced by the reformist Nagy. Nagy tried hard to gain control of the movement, but ended up by being swept along by it. On 30 October he announced a return to a multi-party system; this was too much for the Soviet leaders, who intervened to put down the rising, and installed János Kádár, a centrist, as head of government.

These events broke the impetus towards de-Stalinization and initiated a move back towards orthodoxy. In February 1958 Nagy was executed. In most of eastern Europe (with the exception of Poland), a new investment drive began, and collectivization was resumed in earnest. Collectivization was more or less completed by 1960 in the GDR, by 1961 in Hungary and Czechoslovakia, by 1962 in Romania and in Bulgaria (where the collectivization drive had already restarted in 1956) by 1958.

In political terms the decade from 1957 to 1967 was a period of notable stability, which was brought to an abrupt end by events in Czechoslovakia. Attention focused on the question of economic reforms, which were discussed in all countries and implemented to some degree in most. In Czechoslovakia there had never really been a de-Stalinization process, and discontent in the party built up as economic performance deteriorated in the early 1960s: indeed, in 1962, growth was actually reported to be negative. In 1963 the leadership was obliged to rehabilitate many of those convicted in the purges, and these added their voices to the pressure for change. A half-hearted economic reform was enacted in early 1967, and discontent amongst writers and students became increasingly public as the Stalinist leader, Novotny, lacked the authority to repress it effectively. Alexander Dubček, the leader of the party in Slovakia, became the voice of the anti-Novotny faction, and in December he replaced Novotny as head of the party, though Novotny remained as President of the Republic until April.

Now popular pressure for change began to mount in much the same way that it had in Poland and Hungary in 1956. A section of the party itself began to call for a new democratization, and Dubček aligned himself with this movement. In April Novotny was replaced as head of state by the reformist Smrkovsky. Dubček launched the slogan 'socialism with a human face', and the party's Action Programme promised an ending of censorship and freedom of the press, which came into effect in June. No return to parliamentary democracy or withdrawal from the Warsaw Pact was advocated, but the whole process represented a scarcely veiled criticism of the existing order of things in eastern Europe. When the calling of an extraordinary congress threatened to make the process irreversible through the election of a new central committee, the USSR decided to intervene.

After August 1968, the 'normalization' of Czechoslovakia was gradual but relentless. Under Husak, the party has been notable for a rigid orthodoxy and attachment to the Soviet Union that invites comparison with the GDR. In both countries, the leadership is thoroughly identified with the Soviets and fears any expression of independence or claim to national distinctiveness. Things have been rather different in Hungary and Poland. In Hungary, Kádár has skilfully extended the limits of permitted reforms, chiefly in the economic sphere, and thereby re-established some credibility with the community. For a generation, the unspoken agreement between party and people has been to accept the lessons of 1956 and not to push for too much; this has formed the basis of some interesting and popular experimentation. In Poland the years since 1968 have been turbulent ones, in which the active political involvement of large numbers of workers, symbolised by Lech Walesa, has been the distinctive feature. In both 1970 and 1976 popular opposition to food price increases brought down the existing leadership of the party, and the development of the independent trade union, Solidarity, in 1980 was something entirely novel. The crisis steadily deepened through the autumn of 1980 and 1981, as the party's authority collapsed, and has been only superficially resolved by the military takeover of December 1981.

In the poorer countries of the region, Romania and Bulgaria, internal dissent has never reached the dimensions of a political crisis. In Bulgaria, Todor Zhivkov has been premier since 1954; the country has strong emotional ties with the USSR and economic links have been built up enthusiastically. Romania has for 25 years pursued an independent foreign policy, refusing to join the Warsaw Pact invasion of Czechoslovakia in 1968 or to condemn China in the same way as the rest, but internally it is notorious for being one of the most repressive regimes in eastern Europe.

In spite of these divergences, the central fact of the politics of eastern Europe remains the dependence of most governments on the Soviet army for their survival. Practically every major question is openly or surreptitiously referred to Moscow for an opinion, and national sentiment in these countries is deeply humiliated by this state of affairs. The combination of nationalist outrage and a yearning for a more democratic, less patronising form of regime will inevitably produce more explosions in the future. Popular anger rarely takes an overt form only because of the effectiveness of repression and the feeling that protest would only end in Soviet intervention. Nevertheless, as the population becomes more educated and urban, active political opposition can only become more frequent. In the USSR socio-economic development is creating strong pressures which will lead to demands for more genuine democracy and accountability, as Gorbachev has recognized. In eastern Europe the element of national humiliation makes the political mixture that much more explosive.

The last occasion on which a clearly co-ordinated economic policy can be observed amongst the east European countries is the investment drive and collectivization campaign of the late 1950s. In matters of reform of the planning mechanism, different countries took different measures at different times, and attempted to learn from each others' experience. The early Polish experiment of 1957–8 did not last long, because Gomułka's natural instincts were always towards centralization. The GDR introduced a 'New Economic System' in 1963, which retained detailed central planning for the most important commodities but introduced important elements of flexibility for enterprises producing and consuming other goods. A price reform of the mid-1960s attempted to bring prices more in line with costs, in order to promote rational decision-making by enterprises.

This was followed by a series of reform measures in the USSR (1965), Bulgaria (1965), Czechoslovakia (1967) and Hungary (1968). Of these, the Hungarian and Czech reforms were the most far-reaching in trying to dispense to a large degree with planning by instruction. The Czech experiment was short-lived, since it was accompanied by political changes unacceptable to the Soviet leadership, and was dismantled soon after the Warsaw Pact invasion of August 1968. The Hungarian measures will be discussed in chapter 6. The Bulgarian reforms were already being revised by 1968, and Romania never really embarked on a course of reform.

In the USSR, the reform retained the system of central planning by instruction; but within this it attempted to reduce the number of instructions received by enterprises, to increase their capacity for independent decision-making and to use profit-related bonuses to induce the desired enterprise behaviour. As in the GDR, prices were adjusted to be more in line with costs, and a capital charge of 6 per cent was introduced for the first time. The problem was that the intentions of the reform were continually sabotaged by the prevalence of the old system. Enterprises still had to respond to instructions from above, even if this was unprofitable for them; materials were often not available for enterprise-determined investments, since these were not part of the plan; profits, and hence bonuses, differed considerably from enterprise to enterprise for reasons which were not obviously related to efficiency. When enterprises did qualify for large bonuses, higher organs were reluctant to pay them out because of suspicions that the enterprise had managed to obtain a low base for bonus calculation by fraudulent means. Thus the reform quickly became discredited and by 1970 was largely a dead letter. In the GDR, too, the reform was at least partially reversed in the early 1970s (Keren, 1973; Granick, 1975). The first wave of reforms, outside Hungary, was by then definitely over, and seems to have killed off the idea that minor elements of decentralization and reliance on the profit motive are sufficient to bring about a radical improvement in the performance of the economy.

Economic growth

The purpose of this section is to discuss the general pattern of growth in European socialist countries, not to attempt the more difficult task of comparing their performance with that of the rest of Europe (for this, see chapter 7). The definition of national income employed in these countries is that of the net material product (NMP). This is a narrower measure than gross domestic product (GDP), because it excludes depreciation and much of the service sector (trade, transport and communications, which used to be regarded as 'non-material' activities, are now usually included in NMP). At least up to the early 1970s, when NMP growth was rather fast, NMP growth rates tend to exceed GDP growth rates, principally because the excluded non-material sector was growing more slowly than the material sector. In recent years this effect has largely disappeared, but there are grounds for believing that the official figures overstate economic growth somewhat, for reasons which are discussed in chapter 7. For the purposes of this section I assume that this distortion has remained constant over time, and ignore it.

Table 2.4 gives some information about growth rates in the Soviet bloc from 1950 to 1986. All countries show a pronounced tendency towards deceleration. The GDR appears to have been comparatively little affected, but Keren (1987) suggests that exaggeration of growth rates may have increased there in the last decade. The deceleration was very marked up to 1965 (with the exception of Romania); then growth rates recovered in the next quinquennium, only to fall back again after 1970. For Poland and Romania, the reacceleration was sustained up to 1975, in both cases by heavy foreign borrowing. Growth was slowest in 1981–2; in the years 1983–6 there was some recovery. Plans for 1986–90 imply growth rates that are similar to those for 1976–80, and much lower than those recorded before 1975. Although growth rates have tended to be highest in the least developed countries (Bulgaria and

Table 2.4 Annual average growth rates of net material product 1950–86 (per cent)

Period	*Bulgaria*	*Czechoslovakia*	*GDR*	*Hungary*	*Poland*	*Romania*	*USSR*
1951–5	12.3	8.2	13.3	5.8	8.6	14.2	11.4
1956–60	9.7	6.9	7.2	6.0	6.6	6.6	9.1
1961–5	6.7	2.0	3.4	4.1	6.2	9.0	6.5
1966–70	8.2	6.8	5.2	6.8	6.0	7.7	7.6
1971–5	7.9	5.7	5.4	6.2	9.8	11.2	5.7
1976–80	6.2	3.7	4.1	3.2	1.6	7.1	4.4
1981–5	3.7	1.8	4.5	1.3	−0.8	4.4	3.6
1986	5.5	3.2	4.3	0.5	4.5	7.3	4.1
Plan 1986–90	5.4	3.5	4.6	2.8–3.2	3.0–3.5	10.3	4.3

Sources: Clarke and Matko (1983), pp. 7–8
Smith (1983), p. 40
UNECE (1980), p. 76; (1985/6), p. 114; (1986/7), p. 116

Table 2.5 Estimates of per capita gross national product in 1980

Country	*Estimated 1980 GNP p. c. ($)*	*As % USA*
GDR	5910	52
Czechoslovakia	4740	42
Hungary	4390	39
Poland	3730	33
Bulgaria	3550	31
Romania	2680	24
USSR	4190	37
Eastern Europe	4043	36
Yugoslavia	2620	23

Source: P. Marer, in US Congress Joint Economic Committee (1986), Vol. 3, p. 607

Romania), the ordering of countries by per capita national income remains much as it was in 1938, as table 2.5 shows.

Table 2.6 measures the growth effort, as reflected in the proportion of national income devoted to investment. This ratio increased steadily in the USSR up to 1975, since when it has remained virtually constant at 30 per cent. In eastern Europe it initially increased very fast, levelling off some time in the 1970s (the precise date varying from country to country). Except for Bulgaria, there were sharp falls in east European investment ratios in the early 1980s, with further falls planned for 1986–90.

Table 2.6 Ratio of gross fixed investment to national income 1950–90 (per cent)

Country	*I/GDP* 1950–9	*I/GDP* 1960–8	*I/NMP* 1966–70	*I/NMP* 1971–5	*I/NMP* 1976–80	*I/NMP* 1981–5	*I/NMP* Plan 1986–90
Bulgaria	15.7	25.8	35.1	35.1	35.4	34.9	38.3
Czechoslovakia	14.9	18.8	31.1	33.7	33.7	29.9	28.3
GDR	13.8	18.7	27.6	28.7	30.6	24.9	21.5
Hungary	18.1	22.7	32.9	35.9	37.2	31.0	29.2
Poland	16.9	21.2	25.3	36.4	30.7	24.6	25.8
Romania	16.4	28.1	28.8	34.1	41.3	36.4	28.9
USSR	15.7	18.8	27.0	29.9	30.3	29.8	30.0

Note: Figures are not comparable across countries because of differences in pricing systems.
Source: UNECE (1971), Part I, p. 16; (1976), Part II, p. 10; (1986/7), p. 154

The general impression that emerges is one of an increasing growth effort producing poorer results as time went on. When, in the 1980s, the effort was reduced, the growth rate plummeted to a clearly unsatisfactory level. Plans for 1986–90 look in some respects optimistic, since except for Bulgaria and the Soviet Union they anticipate growth rates similar to 1976–80 on the basis of much lower investment ratios, but do not seem unreasonable if judged by performance over the period 1983–6.

If we look at output in relation to the stock of fixed assets, here too we find that an unfavourable trend has developed. Whereas in the earlier period capital productivity (output per unit of capital) was increasing, except in the Soviet Union, recently the trend has been uniformly negative, as table 2.7 illustrates. The severity of this trend is rather greater than in the capitalist countries.[2] Attempts to fit production functions to the data for these countries since 1970 have frequently emerged with the result that technical progress has ground to a halt. This seems a little unlikely, and may partly result from exaggeration of growth rates of the capital stock (to an even greater degree than output). In any case these results must be treated with caution, since their statistical properties are poor (Cameron, 1981; UNECE, 1985/6).

It is widely believed that Soviet-type economies have severe difficulties in making the transition from an extensive to an intensive pattern of growth. They are very effective at mobilizing investment resources at an early stage of industrialization, when they can increase output rapidly by building new, modern factories to absorb the surplus agricultural population. Once the reserves of labour in agriculture have been exhausted,

Table 2.7 Annual average growth of capital productivity 1950–86 (per cent)

Country	*1950/2–67/9*	*1971–5*	*1976–80*	*1981–5*	*1986*
Bulgaria	0.2	−1.0	−1.8	−3.1	0.4
Czechoslovakia	1.5	−0.1	−1.9	−3.4	−2.4
GDR	2.8	−0.4	−1.5	−0.4	0.5
Hungary	0.7	−2.9	−3.1	−3.1	−3.0
Poland	2.6	1.9	−5.5	−3.4	2.7
Romania	1.0	1.1	−2.9	−4.2	–
USSR	−1.1	−2.8	−2.9	−1.8	−1.5

Source: UNECE (1971), Part I, p. 15; (1981), p. 139; (1986/7), p. 120

the transfer effect disappears and growth comes to depend on improvements in industrial efficiency. This appears to be an area of difficulty for Soviet-bloc economies, as indeed plan fulfilment reports frequently acknowledge. Possible reasons for this will be discussed in chapter 4.

On top of this, some shorter-term factors have been at work. Until 1973 the foreign trade of east European countries was in approximate balance. Then substantial credit became available from western banks on easy terms; this credit was used to finance additional imports and shortfalls in exports. Between 1973 and 1980 eastern Europe built up a substantial foreign debt. Around 1980 there was an abrupt change of policy, caused by a combination of rising real interest rates and alarm at the size of the debt, and strong corrective measures were taken. Imports were cut back sharply, and since 1982 the Soviet bloc has run a significant balance of payments surplus. Over the years 1978 to 1982 growth rates dipped very badly, initially because of poor harvests, but in 1981–2 mainly because of the adjustment problems caused by the reductions in imports. It is probably significant that the USSR, which was enjoying terms of trade gains as an oil exporter at this time, did not experience the same collapse of growth.

Investment cycles

Trade cycles are a well-known feature of capitalist economies, where the proximate influence is effective demand. A centrally planned economy can in theory eliminate such cycles, because it can plan for continuous full employment of resources. It can avoid large fluctuations in investment, or if it wishes to make any rapid alterations, it can eliminate the multiplier effects by rapidly redistributing labour and adjusting wages, prices and taxes so that unemployment or overheating does not develop.

Table 2.8 Industrial production in the USSR (official figures) 1929–40

	Percentage increase over previous year		
Year	*Total*	*Producer goods*	*Consumer goods*
1929	19.7	29.0	14.2
1930	22.2	38.0	10.2
1931	20.7	28.6	13.2
1932	14.6	19.4	9.4
1933	5.2	6.1	4.8
1934	19.2	25.1	12.2
1935	22.7	26.6	17.3
1936	28.7	31.0	25.6
1937	11.2	8.5	15.1
1938	11.7	12.3	11.3
1939	16.1	18.9	11.8
1940	11.7	14.9	7.1

Source: Clarke and Matko (1983), p. 10

But this is just theory. In practice quite a literature has grown up on macroeconomic cycles in centrally planned economies. This is because the rate of growth has shown quite marked historical fluctuations. Even if no one is officially unemployed, output can vary according to the intensity of labour and the quantity of overtime and secondary work which is done.

Theorists of cycles in socialist economies have focused on the propensity towards over-investment as the chief cause, meaning a tendency towards a rate of investment which cannot be sustained for more than a few years because it creates politically intolerable pressure on real incomes, shortages of consumer goods, balance of payments deficits or a build-up of uncompleted projects. Possible sources of such a propensity to over-investment will be discussed in chapters 3 and 4; suffice it to say here that it has a political component, derived from the ambitions of the political leadership, and an economic one, reflecting the relationship between the planners and the enterprise in matters of investment (for a good discussion, see Bauer, 1978). Such a tendency was already clear in the earliest Five-Year Plans of the USSR, as table 2.8 shows. The strains created by striving for very high rates of growth in 1929–32 led to a decision to concentrate on completing existing projects in 1933. Then, after the pause, the investment rate was pushed up again. There was another slowdown in 1937, followed by a further acceleration in 1938–9. This experience suggests a cycle of four to five years.

After 1945, investment cycles are not very apparent in the USSR, but there is quite striking evidence of them in the rest of eastern Europe. There were strong investment drives in 1950–1, which depressed consumption, and cutbacks were made from 1953–4. A new investment drive began in 1958 and lasted until 1960, after which a slowdown ensued, which is clearly visible in table 2.4. Authors writing in the years around 1970 (UNECE, 1969; Bajt, 1971) identified a cycle of about eight years, with a tendency towards a reduction in amplitude. The strong international synchronization reflected the dominance of Soviet influence in the 1950s. The reduction in amplitude might be interpreted as learning by experience on the part of the planners; but it is possible that the investment cycle is a characteristically Stalinist phenomenon, which we can no longer expect to observe in its pristine form. The one clear example from later years is Poland from 1970 to 1976, and this could be regarded as exceptional because it was so obviously related to the political crisis of December 1970 and had no counterpart elsewhere. In most countries development was fairly smooth from 1965 to 1977. Then in eastern Europe deteriorating terms of trade set off a marked cyclical downturn from 1978 to 1982, with recovery beginning in 1983. This cycle was unusual in being initiated by a negative external shock rather than a positive internal one. Clearly, quite an elaborate theory is required to cover all the possible varieties of fluctuation in a socialist economy, taking fully into account the tautness of consumption and balance of payments constraints. As Bauer (1978) points out, it is possible for an investment cycle to exist, but to be confined by the planners to the investment sector. The planners can do this by refusing to alter the investment ratio, so that if it is found that too many investment projects have been approved and their completion is being delayed, the planners do not increase the resources available for investment but simply cut the 'approval coefficient' until the projects already under way are finished.

Agriculture

The remainder of this chapter will focus on the agricultural sector. Industrial organization will be discussed in chapter 3, in connection with the planning system. Agriculture deserves a measure of special attention for a number of reasons. First, the agricultural sector is larger than in the advanced capitalist economies; secondly, it retains unique organizational features, which reflect the historical confrontation between a socialist state and small peasant farming; and thirdly, it has traditionally been and continues to be a problem sector for socialist economies.

As already mentioned, the collectivization drive in eastern Europe was more or less halted in the period immediately following Stalin's death. In

Poland and Yugoslavia, the peasants were given the opportunity to leave the collective farms, and no subsequent attempt was made to collectivize by coercion. Consequently the agriculture of these two countries remains dominated by small peasant farming, and the remarks below do not apply to them. Elsewhere, the hardening of the political line in the late 1950s created pressure to complete the collectivization process, which was duly achieved within a few years. This time, the characteristically Stalinist element of 'dekulakization' (sharply discriminatory measures against richer peasants), which had led to some land simply being abandoned in the early 1950s, was less evident. The organization of collective farms followed the Soviet model closely. The peasants were allowed to retain private plots of similar size to those permitted in the USSR, and could keep similar quantities of livestock. Remuneration of farm members followed the Soviet system of labour day units. The Soviet dismantling of the Machine Tractor Stations was likewise imitated in most countries (the exceptions were Romania and Albania).

In the early 1950s the economic development of agriculture was largely neglected, as investment resources were concentrated in heavy industry. Agricultural output did not reach its pre-war level until 1957 in eastern Europe, and about 1955 in the USSR. Since then there has been steady growth, and a considerable increase in per capita consumption of higher quality foods such as meat and dairy products, but the supply of food has often been insufficient to match the demand. This is because real incomes have risen steadily and the demand for meat is income elastic, whilst the authorities have often been reluctant, for political reasons, to raise the price. In the USSR food subsidies (chiefly for meat, dairy and baking products) took up no less than 12 per cent of the state budget in the mid-1980s. By then the price of these subsidized products had remained unchanged for 20 years, and since the rate of inflation, though low, is not zero, their relative price had steadily fallen.

Nevertheless, these demand factors cannot disguise the fact that the performance of the agricultural sector has tended to be unsatisfactory. Only in the GDR is agricultural labour productivity comparable with the rest of the economy; elsewhere it lags far behind, although agriculture is not obviously undercapitalized (Wädekin, 1982, pp. 109–13).

Agriculture in these countries has certainly been the victim of deficiencies in the planning system. For example, it is often commented in the USSR that a far from negligible proportion of agricultural output is lost in being transported in open-top lorries along appallingly maintained roads, and Ellman (1986) refers to estimates that anything from 20 to 50 per cent of the crop is unnecessarily spoiled or wasted. The livestock sector has suffered from an insufficiency of proteins in animal diets. If

Table 2.9 Average farm size in the USSR 1937–65

	Collective farms		*State farms*	
Year	*Hectares agricultural land*	*No. of households*	*Hectares agricultural land*	*No. of workers*
1937	1534	76	12,200	285
1953	4211	220	13,100	352
1965	6100	420	24,600	653

Source: Wädekin (1982), p. 50

agricultural machinery breaks down, its repair is often delayed by a lack of spare parts. Fertilisers may not arrive at the appropriate time. Because agriculture is inherently a seasonal activity, the timing of inputs is critical, and late arrival of supplies is frequently equivalent to non-delivery.

But problems with supply of inputs from outside agriculture is only a part of the story. Whereas in the west farming is a small capitalist, if not peasant, activity, in the east the cult of bigness prevails. This was evident from the very first days of collectivization, when the activities of Gigant, an enormous collective farm in the Urals, were given great prominence in the press. Industrialization of agriculture, its conversion to factory methods and social relationships, is the aim which tends to be regarded, especially in the USSR, as synonymous with socialism. Table 2.9 illustrates the tendency towards larger and larger collective farms. By 1960 collective farms had already attained roughly their present size in Bulgaria and the USSR, but in Czechoslovakia, Hungary and Romania, where farms were on average much smaller in 1960, farm size has grown rapidly towards the Soviet figure, which seems to be currently regarded as optimal for lowland regions.

But even this is not the end of the story. In the 1950s Khrushchev advocated the creation of 'agro-towns' to replace villages. The idea was rejected at the time because of the cost in new housing and services, but it has never died entirely. Investment decisions in the countryside continue to reflect this sort of thinking. 'The whole logic of the collective farm involves the death of the old Russian village and the community which sustained it. In the region of Perm, for example, the plan published in 1980 listed 5642 rural centres, and 5170 were condemned to lingering death by the year 2000 as officially 'without future' as the population is shifted into larger economic centres' (Martin Walker, *The Guardian*, 31 December 1986).

The destruction of the village would also mean the end of the private plot, which normally consists of an area immediately surrounding the farmer's house, as the agricultural population is moved into urban flats; indeed this is almost certainly the political intention behind the idea.

A collective farm consisting of hundreds of households is necessarily a bureaucratic organization. In Stalin's time the motivation of collective farmers was very low because the income of the collective was squeezed by low producer prices; at the margin, it was infinitely more rewarding to put effort into one's private plot. Since Stalin's death remuneration of collective farm work has improved immeasurably, but the incentive effect is reduced by the fact that each individual represents less than 1 per cent of the farm's labour force. The impact on collective farm income of more intensive work by one individual is negligible. The result is a marked tendency towards inattentiveness, sloppy habits and an unwillingness to put in the extra hour of work here and there which may be of crucial importance in harvesting or the care of animals. At the margin, individual effort on the collective farm still has an effective return of zero. In addition, the bureaucratic structure of a large organization creates difficulties. The timing of labour inputs needs to be adapted to weather conditions and circumstances; the small enterprise continues to dominate in the west precisely because it facilitates this. In the collective farms of the east, bureaucratic considerations often inhibit the required flexibility.

In response to this Gorbachev has recently espoused the brigade system, an idea with a long history in Soviet agriculture and which has received some official support in the whole Soviet economy since 1979 (Gagnon, 1987). In agriculture, this would involve a brigade of workers taking responsibility for cultivation of a field for a season, hiring materials from the collective farm, and being paid according to results. There are many administrative problems concerning what production 'norms' to apply, what rates of pay to establish and so on, and it is still too early to say whether this will amount to a significant change in the workings of the agricultural sector.

The collective farm represents a lower degree of socialization than the state farm, which employs wage labour on a similar basis to the industrial sector. In the USSR, it has been the policy for some time to convert collective farms into state farms. In 1960 collective farms covered 56.4 per cent of the agricultural area; by 1978 they covered only 31.9 per cent (Wädekin, 1982, p. 85). The change has been slow because of the disadvantage that state farms tend to operate at a loss and are a drain on the budget; to counter this, wage payments on state farms have been tied to results. No such policy operates in eastern Europe, except in Bulgaria, but in all countries the differences between state and collective farms have tended to diminish. This has been accomplished in a variety of ways. Collective farmers receive a lower proportion of their income in kind than before, and now normally receive a regular monthly or quarterly advance on their annual income, which is akin to a guaranteed wage. The gap in pay between collective and state farms is being closed, and collective farmers have slowly been brought into the social insurance network. State pensions for collective farmers already existed in some east European countries in the 1950s, and the USSR introduced them in 1965.

Thus the tendency has been towards a more uniform agricultural sector, based on large units, in which it is hoped that the private plot will diminish in significance and ultimately wither away. The stress in recent years has been on an effective linking of agriculture with processing industry. Considerable demands have been placed on agriculture by rising real incomes and a policy of low food prices, and so far the performance of the highly socialized system seems clearly inferior to that of the smaller private farms of western countries. The title of a recent book on Hungarian agriculture, *Collective Farms which Work?* is eloquent testimony to a widespread judgement that they do not.

Notes

1 The political element in this decision is often overlooked by western writers. According to the émigré Fyodor Kushnirsky (1982, p. 51), the desire to clip the wings of local party apparatuses and centralize power in Moscow was the major motivation.

2 It may in part be a statistical artifact, resulting from a higher rate of hidden inflation in the field of investment goods production than elsewhere. This will be discussed further in chapter 7.

3

Planners and Enterprises

The construction of a plan

This chapter describes the operation of the planning system as developed in the USSR in the 1930s, and which, in essence, continues to operate in that country and most of the others in eastern Europe to this day, despite episodes of 'reform'. The fundamental principle of the system is that it is a hierarchical one, in which the enterprise receives instructions from above which have the force of law (the Hungarian system, which since 1968 has dispensed to a large degree with planning by instruction, is discussed in chapter 6). These instructions cover the outputs which the enterprise is expected to produce over a certain period and the inputs which it is allowed to use, and may also contain a large number of other targets. The degree of detail varies greatly depending on the prevailing philosophy of the moment; instructions relating to labour, for example, may specify precisely how much labour of various types may be employed and at what average wage, or only a very general indicator such as the total wage bill. With few exceptions prices and wages are set centrally, and it is part of the job of the banking system to ensure that the enterprise's expenditures are in accordance with its plan.

The central planners do not deal directly with individual enterprises; they break the plan down by ministry, and the ministry then allocates its plan totals amongst the enterprises under its control. In recent decades an additional tier in the planning hierarchy has become more significant: that of the industrial association, a grouping of a few enterprises in a similar field of activity. Industrial associations have some of the characteristics of a kind of super-enterprise, and some of the characteristics of a government office, so that it is not easy to summarize their functions (for a useful discussion see Zielinski, 1973, especially chapter 8), and in what follows the discussion will be only in terms of enterprises and ministries (this is not a drastic oversimplification since the essential issues concern the relationships between superiors and subordinates at whatever level in the planning hierarchy). The development of industrial associations is best regarded as an attempt to decentralize decision-taking somewhat *within* the administrative framework of planning by instruction, without giving enterprises much greater *economic* freedom.

The enterprise is owned by the state, and its profits accrue to the state. For a long period, the enterprise was not charged for its capital stock; investment funds were allocated free. More recently, however (since 1965 in the USSR), it has become normal for the enterprise to have to pay a rental charge on its capital. An investment project of any size has to be submitted to the higher bodies for authorization, and only if it is included in the planned total of investments for that year will the funds be provided for it.

The fundamental point, therefore, is that the enterprise has rather little freedom of manoeuvre. It cannot take any major decisions unless these have been incorporated into the enterprise plan. It signs purchasing and sales contracts with other enterprises, but only on the basis of its plan instructions, and the enterprise is liable to receive orders from the ministry at any time, specifying how the plan is to be carried out and not infrequently requiring the enterprise to do things which are not consistent with the published plan. It is easy to see that this system places an immense burden on the planning organizations. They have to draw up a plan which will ensure that every enterprise can obtain the inputs which it needs, and that it produces output that is needed by someone else. They also have to ensure that the transport system can get the goods from supplier to customer at the requisite time. Supply and demand are not equalized through the price mechanism, since prices are for the most part fixed. It is the planners who have to achieve this.

The problem would appear to lend itself to input-output analysis of the kind familiar from any textbook in mathematical economics. If we assume constant returns to scale, and we know the inputs used and outputs produced by each enterprise, then input-output analysis allows us to estimate the gross outputs required to satisfy any particular level of final demand. In practice, planners in the USSR and eastern Europe have never used the input-output method to draw up an *operational* plan (an operational plan is one which is broken down to enterprise level and sent to enterprises as an instruction). The reason is that it has some serious practical disadvantages.

First, it assumes that each commodity is produced using the same inputs per unit of output in each enterprise. In reality enterprises differ with respect to the quality of their machinery, climatic conditions and location, and their inputs per unit of output may vary because they produce different types within a given commodity range. Secondly, input-output analysis provides only an aggregate solution; it does not solve the problem of what each enterprise should produce, to whom it should be delivered or from whom its inputs should be obtained. Thus there is a transportation problem which needs to be solved simultaneously with the production problem. Finally, when firms produce more than one product, as is frequently the case, the rigid assumptions of input-output analysis can easily generate ridiculous solutions if some information is lacking or if commodities are not sufficiently disaggregated.

In short, the input-output approach is too abstract and theoretical, and does not make efficient use of information available at enterprise level, but not to the planners, as a check against absurd solutions (for further discussion of this, see Tretyakova and Birman, 1976). It is useful to the planners in longer-term macroeconomic planning, and is increasingly being used for these purposes, but not for detailed microeconomic problems.

Thus annual and quarterly plans are based on what is known as the materials balance approach. This involves a complex interaction between planners and enterprises, in which the plan goes through a series of drafts and, in fact, is not usually finally adopted until after the plan period to which it refers has begun. The process starts with the planners drawing up a draft plan, which will be based on the expected outcome for the current year, with some growth added in. In response to this the enterprises communicate back to the planners their input requirements. When aggregated, this gives the planners a picture of the total supply and demand of every commodity which is used as an input. Since enterprises would like 'slack' plans (ones which are easier to fulfil), there is a tendency for demand to exceed supply. The planners try to combat this and to impose plan tautness through the use of national norms and by refusing to allow inputs (especially of labour) to increase at the same rate as outputs. Juggling with the figures in the light of these considerations, the planners come up with a second draft plan, and the cycle is repeated. Typically, in the USSR, the process starts in the middle of the year before the one to which the plan refers, but is completed after the beginning of the plan year. This does not leave time for more than two or three iterations (for further discussion see Kushnirsky, 1982, chapter 3). If the planners were starting from a random point, the attempt to solve such an input-output problem by trial and error using only a small number of iterations would not get close to a consistent solution: the plan would contain many imbalances. But because the planners are able to use the previous year's results as a basis, their first draft is a good approximation to the final result, and the errors which remain after a few iterations are much smaller (Hare, 1981).

Nevertheless this does not prevent the plan from containing many errors. Though the planners can and do attempt to regulate the volume of consumer demand through the enterprise wage bill, they cannot determine its distribution amongst products. Since households are remunerated predominantly in money, and prices are fixed in advance, the distribution of consumer demand can only be forecast. Equally, because there is free choice of occupation and place of work, some enterprises may suffer chronic labour shortages. If a factory is not completed on time, its planned output does not appear. An accident, such as the Chernobyl disaster, may cause considerable disruption.

A more fundamental problem than any of these sources of uncertainty is that the central planners can only deal with products aggregated into broad categories. In the 1981 annual plan for the USSR, the State Planning Commission constructed balances for 2044 products, the State Committee on Supply 7500 and individual ministries 25000 (Schroeder, 1982, p. 75). This seems to add up to an impressive number, until one begins to consider the quantity of products handled by a large builder's merchant or supermarket in the west. Indeed it has been calculated that price lists in the USSR contain 12 million different items (Nove et al., 1982, p. 32). The plan cannot possibly cover every size and variety of screw; at best it can deal with screws in the aggregate, summed by mass or value. In order to obtain the right assortment of screws, the system relies on detailed contracts between customers and suppliers. Potentially, this gives the customer an important sanction against the supplier, since enterprises can be sued for non-fulfilment of contracts. This sanction is greatly weakened, however, by the difficulty experienced by the customer in specifying in sufficient detail the exact nature and timing of its requirements over the next year.

Alongside the physical plan runs a financial plan. One of the chief functions of the financial plan is to balance the consumer goods market. By controlling total expenditure on wages and bonuses, the planners attempt to keep the volume of consumer demand equal to the supply of consumer goods forthcoming at prevailing prices. The banking system plays an important policing role here. Enterprises are only allowed to draw cash in order to pay wages; payments to other enterprises must be made by cheque. Thus the state bank can directly oversee an enterprise's wage bill through its cash withdrawals and ensure that it does not exceed the plan. In order to make payments to others, an enterprise must prove to the bank that such a payment is authorized in the plan, by presenting an allocation certificate entitling it to the materials purchased. As far as inter-enterprise transfers are concerned, this is a 'documentary' economy: nothing can be done without the necessary documents; money on its own is not sufficient. This explains why enterprises which are in desperate need of materials not included in their plan allocation have to resort to complicated forms of barter.

The state budget finances administration, the social services, defence and also the bulk of investment. In the USSR about half of budget expenditure falls under the category of 'national economy', a catch-all which includes investment but also a large number of rather obscure items (Nove, 1977, pp. 237–9). The bulk of budget revenue comes from the turnover tax and charges on enterprise profits. Direct taxation plays a rather small role, and income tax rates are low relative to those prevailing in western Europe. This is because the state has so much control over pre-tax income that the redistributive function of income tax is largely redundant. Turnover tax is not set at prescribed rates; it is simply the difference between the price charged to the consumer and that paid to producing and distributing enterprises. The rate of tax often varies greatly from one good to another, and for many years it has been strongly negative on state housing and a number of basic food products.

In principle all enterprise profits accrue to the state. The question is how much the enterprise is permitted to retain to spend on individual bonuses, collective services for employees and enterprise-determined productive investment. Because of irrationalities in the pricing system, it has always been the case that enterprises in some sectors have been loss-making, whereas in others they have been highly profitable. One of the objects of periodic price reforms has been to reduce this, and the USSR is currently attempting to make enterprises in a whole number of consumer goods industries self-financing. Since major price reforms only occur every 15–20 years, and between the reforms relative prices steadily diverge from costs, this objective seems fanciful in the absence of any radical moves towards price flexibility. When prices are revised, the principle invariably used is to base prices on costs plus some mark-up for profits.

It should already be clear from what has been said that the planners do not have the information to accomplish their task in the manner that they would like. They have to aggregate, to improvise and to troubleshoot as shortages and bottlenecks arise. Thus, although the system employs a central planning mechanism in which enterprises receive categorical instructions on the most important questions, nevertheless they enjoy a certain freedom which stems from the planners' shortage of exact information about their capacities. Enterprise managers can use their informational advantage to influence the plans they receive to suit themselves, and the resulting behaviour may frustrate the planners' intentions. The whole question of economic reform centres around the problem of how to make the private interests of those working in the enterprise coincide with the social interest as perceived by the planners. From the very earliest days bonuses have been offered for plan fulfilment. But what exactly constitutes successful fulfilment of the plan?

Success indicators

This is the problem of 'success indicators'. Such indicators are inevitably biased towards what is easily identifiable and measurable. It is easier to measure the total output of an enterprise than to estimate the quality of the product, or whether the assortment of goods has met the needs of customers. If the enterprise is struggling to meet the plan, it may choose to sacrifice assortment or quality for volume, even though it leaves the customers dissatisfied, because it thereby fulfils the success criteria of the higher authorities. This behaviour has long been complained about in the Soviet press, whence it has been faithfully reproduced in western books and articles. Since these press items are deliberately agitational, they can seldom be relied on to give a rounded picture of the matter. It is the frequency of similar complaints over wide areas of the economy, rather than the contents of any one article, which give an indication of the scale of the problems. One of the few systematic studies of the Stalinist model of central planning available in English is János Kornai's *Overcentralisation in Economic Administration* (1959). This is the report of a research study of Hungarian light industry (mainly textiles and leatherware) in 1955. It illustrates very clearly how enterprises respond in Pavlovian fashion to the success indicators which are offered to them. The next few paragraphs summarise the main results of Kornai's study, which coincide very closely with the conclusions of observers of the Soviet economy at the same date.

1 The enterprise's time horizon is no longer than the next plan deadline. In Hungary in the mid-1950s the relevant operational plans were quarterly. Annual plans were formulated, but were virtually ignored by enterprise managers. In the same way, five-year plans in the USSR have no importance to enterprises, whose performance is judged according to annual or quarterly targets. Longer-term plans are ignored because they cannot in practice be taken as accurate forecasts of future operational plans, although this is their theoretical role.

2 The need for aggregation in measures of gross output creates opportunities for enterprises to make their plans easier to fulfil by a favourable assortment of goods. If gross output is specified in value terms, as in the Hungarian case, enterprises favour products with a high

price but low value added, that is those using a greater volume or a higher quality of raw materials. Products which demand disproportionate effort by the enterprise per unit value of output figure disproportionately in plan shortfalls. This phenomenon is very well known in the Soviet Union. Transport organizations whose plans are specified in ton kilometres dislike short hauls because their plans make no allowance for loading times; pipe-laying enterprises fail to lay pipes to sufficient depth if only the length of pipe figures in the plan; and so on.

3 If cost of production is made an important plan indicator, as in Hungary after 1954 and in the USSR from 1959 to 1965, enterprises may sacrifice quality to achieve this target by using cheaper materials or poorer quality.

4 If unsold stocks count towards output, enterprises may worry little about whether their output is saleable. In Hungary this was a particular problem for above-plan output, which was not covered by any sales contract. In 1965 the USSR brought in a new regulation that only sold output should count towards plan fulfilment, in order to combat this.

5 If work in progress counts towards output, enterprises may be tempted to use some device to turn raw materials into 'semi-finished products' at little cost, by simply carrying out the first stage of production. In the Hungarian leather industry this was achieved by throwing large numbers of hides into the vat for soaking.

6 If, as in the traditional system, no managerial bonuses are paid if the plan is not fulfilled, there is very little incentive to maximize production once a shortfall becomes inevitable; indeed the incentive is then to count some of this period's output as next period's, in order to increase the chances of fulfilling next period's plan.

In general, managers orient themselves to those success indicators which carry the greatest bonuses and which may be taken to indicate the priorities of the higher authorities, relegating other indicators to a secondary role. An example of this, common in the USSR, is the practice of 'storming'. Storming means production at a hectic rate towards the end of a plan period in a desperate rush to fulfil the output plan, neglecting all other considerations such as quality, maintenance of equipment and, in general, any other postponable task. Here is a report from a British journalist in the USSR in 1984 (Walker, 1986, p. 42):

> 'We never use a screwdriver in the last week', one production line worker at a Lithuanian television factory told me. 'We hammer the screws in. We slam solder on the connections, cannibalise parts from other TVs if we have run out of the right ones, use glue or hammers to fix switches that were never meant for that model. And

all the time management is pressing us to work faster, to make the target so we all get our bonuses.'

The fact that a fair proportion of the output produced in such a storming session may subsequently be returned by customers because of defects makes little difference to behaviour, because it happens only after a certain lapse of time and so affects only the next period's output figures.

These examples are sufficient to indicate the problems faced by the planners in designing success indicators. The difficulties are of two types: (1) some aspects of performance are difficult to quantify; and (2) good performance is a multi-dimensional entity. Under (1) the problems of measuring quality and attentiveness to the requirements of customers have already been mentioned. Under (2) the problem is to find a way of getting the enterprises to put appropriate weight on all the various aspects of good performance. Kornai (1959, p. 121) lists these as follows:

The six most important *desiderata* are that production be carried on so that:

1 current and embodied labour inputs should be as small as possible;
2 with the minimum practicable use of fixed equipment and circulating capital;
3 in producing articles of the highest possible quality;
4 in as large quantities as possible;
5 these products being those that are most needed by society;
6 all this being done in such a way as not to endanger future production, but rather to promote it.

This last category would include such matters as proper maintenance and care of equipment, and achieving a desirable rate of technical innovation. The traditional approach is to issue detailed plan instructions covering all these matters. The question then is whether all such aspects of performance are closely monitored. To do so, and to check all figures provided by enterprises, puts a great strain on administrative resources. If bonuses were made conditional on all plan indices being successfully fulfilled, so few enterprises would qualify that the whole system of incentives would be undermined. If bonuses are a complex function of plan indicators, not only is the administrative cost high but selection of the appropriate coefficients becomes a highly complex matter.

In practice there are powerful forces tending to make two or three plan indicators of much greater importance than the rest. First amongst these is the fact that total output will almost inevitably have pride of place. This occurs partly because the plan is the subject of political agitation and propaganda to stimulate effort, and output targets are the best focus for this (the most extreme version of this kind of agitation was the Stakhanovite movement of the 1930s). A further reason for the importance of total output is that a shortfall in this area is likely to impair plan fulfilment of others who need that output as inputs (the same could be said of assortment or quality, but in these cases at least the customer is offered something). A second factor leading to the predominance of two or three indicators is the involvement of the political leadership in the plan. There is a tendency for politicians to treat economic policy as crisis management, emphasizing one or two objectives at a time and neglecting others which are for the moment politically 'invisible' (Blackaby, 1978).

Finally, even if a bonus system incorporates all the variables thought to be desirable, and is appropriately adjusted to allow for the different technical conditions in different industries (itself a considerable administrative task), it cannot eliminate undesirable forms of behaviour because it cannot allow for the very different trade-offs facing the enterprise at different moments in the plan cycle: plan formulation, the outset of the plan period, and the approach of the deadline. As the plan period progresses the enterprise becomes increasingly myopic, and carries a greater and greater burden of past performance for which its decisions in the rest of plan period must compensate. This burden of the past has no equivalent in capitalist economies. A capitalist firm hit by a strike is not thereby induced to make radical sacrifices in quality for quantity when production is resumed. Under central planning such storming behaviour arises because of the need to compensate for lost production earlier in the plan period, and no bonus function which attaches any significant weight to output could prevent it.[1] Thus there is no such thing as a perfect bonus system which can eliminate all undesirable forms of behaviour. The authorities recognise this and prefer to go for a relatively simple, comprehensible bonus system which expresses their main priorities, and to resort to moral exhortation for the rest.

Enterprise reactions to supply difficulties

As just mentioned, an enterprise not infrequently finds its production programme threatened by a shortage of raw materials, either because of a plan error, below-plan production at another plant, diversion of shipments to a higher priority customer or for some other reason. Not infrequently the enterprise has to indulge in 'forced substitution' of the materials that are at hand for those that are missing. The official planning apparatus contains no mechanism for helping an enterprise in such a difficulty, other than to make complaints to higher authorities. Enterprises are not allowed to make public offers to buy the deficient materials, since the seller would have no plan instruction to sell them and payment would not be authorized. However this restriction can be evaded by entering into barter deals. One enterprise telephones others to find one which can spare the needed materials, and in exchange offers, or offers to obtain, something required by the supplier. Chains of barter may be built up in this way. Enterprises frequently employ 'expediters' or 'fixers' (*tolkachi* in Russian) who specialize in knowing how and where to obtain things. Such exchanges are strictly illegal, but are tolerated because they perform a useful function: they redistribute resources from places where they are temporarily idle to points where they are desperately needed. Indeed it is in the interest of a ministry to help its subordinate enterprises to conclude this sort of deal, because the ministry's own plan is the sum of that of all the enterprises under its command.

Once the enterprise has secured a plan which appears feasible with the resources allocated to it, the greatest danger is that the materials for which it has contracted will not arrive on time. One way to deal with this is to try to build in to the plan allocation a superfluous quantity of materials, so that over time substantial reserve stocks may be accumulated. However, this cannot always be relied on, because the planners are always trying to counteract this tendency, and past delivery shortfalls may have prevented it. A second form of insurance is to try to reduce reliance on outside suppliers, by producing as much as possible 'in house'. This is known as the tendency to self-supply.

At enterprise level, this could take the form of actual production of its own inputs, or just emergency facilities which are not normally used. Nevertheless, the scope for such 'self-supply' within an enterprise may well be limited, and confined to spare parts for machinery or relatively small items. According to a 1966 Soviet article quoted by Berliner (1976, p. 72), a staggering 90 per cent of all spare parts are produced to order in the machine shops of the *using* enterprise, rather than bought from the producers of the equipment.

At ministry level, self-supply can take a more substantial form, with the ministry actually setting up plants to supply the whole of its enterprises' requirements for some commodity, rather than having to depend on another ministry with a poor delivery record. This is likely to generate wasteful duplication of production facilities and unnecessary transportation, since the ministry's own source of supply may be much further away from some of the customer enterprises than the nearest alternative source. Thus the general effect of self-supply is excessive transport costs and inefficient small-scale production outside of specialist plants. In the period from 1957 to 1965, when the USSR went over from a ministerial to a regional planning system, self-supply was reflected in the desire of each region to have its own cement factory, steel combine and so on, rather than import these commodities from another region.

The pressure towards self-supply also has important effects on foreign trade. The planners do not wish to make their own plan fulfilment dependent on the arrivals of supplies from abroad unless there are pressing reasons for doing so. This means that they will try to import only those things which would be very costly or impossible to produce at home, such as primary products and advanced western machinery. Unlike in capitalist economies, where firms often find it profitable to launch an export drive in order to break into foreign markets, there is no intrinsic benefit to the socialist enterprise or the planners in increasing exports. Foreign trade is therefore import-led, and dominated by imports for which there are no good home substitutes.

Trade amongst socialist countries is organized largely under the auspices of the Council for Mutual Economic Assistance (CMEA). Within CMEA trade is mostly on a bilateral basis, and the accounting unit is the transferable rouble. Since neither this nor the domestic currencies of east European countries are convertible, a surplus on CMEA trade cannot be used to pay for imports from outside CMEA.

As mentioned above, the priority within CMEA is to mesh in with the domestic planning process. Broad categories of exports and imports for a Five-Year Plan period are negotiated between the foreign trade ministries of the countries concerned, and are fleshed out in detail later. In order to avoid awkward choices over prices, a rule has been evolved whereby prices are based on the world market average over the previous five years, though the precise application of this rule is also the subject of detailed negotiation. It is the complexity of the negotiation process which inhibits the growth of multilateral trading within CMEA, for multilateralism would require two-sided negotiations, which are already complicated enough, to become many-sided ones. On any statistical measure, the degree of multilateralism in intra-CMEA trade is indeed very low, not only relative to that of western Europe, but even in relation to CMEA members' trade with outsiders (Smith, 1983, pp. 157–63). Effectively, extra imports from another CMEA member have to be paid for, more or less immediately, by additional exports to that member. Other things being equal, it will therefore always be preferable to export outside CMEA and earn hard currency. Within CMEA, the tendency is to offer exports which are of insufficient quality to be saleable on western markets; or in other words, to offer what the importer can be persuaded to accept. Knowledge of this combines with the preference for self-supply to inhibit the interchange of industrial products within CMEA.

Planning from the achieved level

So far little has been said about an important aspect of the planning system: how enterprises take account of the future. Because operational plans are short (quarterly or annual) and represent the main criterion by which enterprise management is judged, enterprises are encouraged to be extremely myopic. The whole phenomenon of storming is an excellent example of this. Nevertheless it would be wrong to conclude from this that anticipations of the future do not influence enterprise behaviour. There is one aspect of the future of which enterprises are particularly aware: the relationship between their performance in the current plan period and the targets they will be given in the next one. Since remuneration is based on plan fulfilment, the enterprise has a clear interest in obtaining a slack plan. For reasons which are discussed below, there tends to be a strong relationship between an enterprise's performance in the current period and its target in the next. The Soviet term for this is planning 'from the achieved level'. The effect is that if an enterprise does very well today, it is penalized tomorrow. A slight overfulfilment of the plan will often be better than a remarkable one, even though it results in a smaller bonus today, because it does not jeopardize future bonuses.

Planning from the achieved level persists, despite the fact that its defects are well known (Birman, 1978). The reason is that the planners lack the information to replace it with any other system. If the planners could make an effective judgement as to how much this period's and previous periods' performance was influenced by quality of management, work effort, weather conditions, supplies of raw materials, age and condition of machinery or any other relevant variable, they might be able to make sensible estimates of these variables in the next period which would take into account any special circumstances pertaining in the current one. In that case the enterprise might be able to perform exceptionally well in one period in the knowledge that the planners were aware that circumstances had been unusually favourable. But the planners could only acquire such information by the most detailed supervision of the enterprise's operations, and this is a luxury they cannot afford. Much effort goes into devising norms for labour productivity and other variables, in order to identify areas of slack in the system, but the applicability of these norms suffers from the enormous variation between enterprises in age and type of equipment and range of products manufactured. To add 4 or 5 per cent to each enterprise's output in the last period is a quick and easy solution to a problem which might not be greatly illuminated by anything but the most intensive investigation. Whilst planning from the achieved level may discourage substantial plan overfulfilment, it is an effective method of building into the plan a permanent change in an enterprise's productivity capacity, provided one can assume that, sooner or later, the improvement will be reflected in enterprise performance. In short, even though its defects in discouraging substantial overfulfilment of plans are well known, the simplicity and cheapness of the method ensure its continued employment.

Enterprise reactions to the practice of planning from the achieved level are just one instance of a much deeper problem: that the desire to obtain slack plans is the only obvious way in which enterprises take the future into account. When the future comes, they may have an interest in many things, but these cannot possibly be known until the plan is formulated. Therefore the only possible objective is to influence the plan in a favourable direction. The most favourable direction tends to be a conservative one. Nothing would be easier for the enterprise than to run along familiar, well-worn grooves, using the same equipment and the same quantity of labour to produce the same products, with materials supplied from established sources. This would minimize the chances of production being disrupted by machinery breakdowns or shortages of materials.

If this seems dubious, consider an enterprise which is approached by a research organization. The researchers say that they have discovered a way of producing a better-quality product, using new machinery and a different set of materials, but at a substantially lower cost. How would the enterprise manager react? Probably the first question that would spring to mind would be: are the planners aware of this innovation and are they intending to incorporate it in my future plan? The second question might be: how many trials has this innovation received? If the project is not being pushed from above and the enterprise is being used as a guinea-pig, it is most unlikely that the manager would be enthusiastic about it. Despite the cost advantage, the difficulties of learning to use new machines, of getting the correct materials allocations written into the next plan, and of finding reliable suppliers of them, are likely to be such that the initial prospects of plan fulfilment would be poor. Moreover the investment would have to be justified to the higher authorities, so that some of the expected benefits would be quickly 'socialized' through higher plan targets. This illustrates the point that the cost advantage in itself is not important to the enterprise; it is the cost change measured against likely alterations in the planned targets for costs which matter.

What this hypothetical example suggests is that in the traditional model of central planning, the enterprise has intrinsically rather little interest in economic progress. Progress has to be imposed on it from above, through plan instructions, orders, campaigns and agitation. This may explain the apparent difficulty experienced by these economies in

Table 3.1 Primary energy consumption per capita (kg. coal equivalent)

Area/Country	*1950*	*1958*	*1969*
Western Europe	1854	2387	3437
Eastern Europe	1826	2490	3592
USSR	1688	2888	4187
USA	6039	7628	10768

Source: UNECE (1971), Part I, p. 87

making the transition from extensive to intensive economic growth, discussed in chapter 2. Intensive growth requires the sort of detailed technical knowledge which the planners lack and only the enterprise possesses. But the enterprises have little interest in revealing these possibilities to the planners.

The hoarding of inputs

The whole question of technical innovation will be discussed in more detail in the next chapter. A slightly different example of a similar phenomenon relates to the use of inputs. There is little incentive for the enterprise to reveal excessive inputs of materials and labour, and underemployment on the job is a well known phenomenon. As a result of investment in new machinery, enterprises record steady improvements in labour productivity, but all the time they may have a labour force 10 or 20 per cent above requirements. Raw materials tend to be used in a profligate fashion because, once allocated, the incentive to conserve them is low. This may be demonstrated by looking at energy statistics. As table 3.1 shows, the USSR and eastern Europe had already overtaken western Europe in per capita energy consumption by 1960, despite their much lower levels of national income. Growth of energy use was especially fast in the USSR, which is well endowed with energy resources. Those who have attempted to estimate the intensity of raw material and energy use in the CMEA countries have suggested that it is now 30–40 per cent above that of the developed capitalist countries (i.e. for each unit of national income produced, 30–40 per cent more units of raw material are used in the east than in the west). In particular, the socialist countries have failed to replace steel by other materials: steel intensity in the CMEA is about three times that of the EEC (UNECE, 1985/6, pp. 125–6).

It is also interesting to compare the response of energy consumption in

Table 3.2 Change in energy consumption per unit of net material product (per cent per annum)

Country	*1976–80*	*1981–4*
Bulgaria	−0.1	−2.3
Czechoslovakia	−0.9	−1.2
GDR	−1.3	−2.2
Hungary	1.4	−1.5
Poland	2.8	1.2
Romania	−2.1	−3.5
USSR	−0.7	−1.5

Source: UNECE (1985/6), p. 127

different countries to the sharp rise in the real price of energy in the 1970s. Whatever the domestic price of energy, the world price still represented the true opportunity cost to the socialist countries, in the form of additional imports (eastern Europe) or exports foregone (USSR). The incentive to conserve energy was therefore just as strong as in the rest of the world. In the seven major countries of the OECD area, energy use per unit of GDP fell between 1973 and 1982 by 11 per cent in the transport sector, 19 per cent in the residential/commercial sector and 31 per cent in industry (the differences reflect variations in the size of the energy price increase to various users, because of tax effects). Broadly, however, one can say that energy intensity declined at about 2 per cent per annum (*OECD Economic Outlook* 33, July 1983, pp. 78–9).

Comparable figures for eastern Europe and the Soviet Union for the period 1976–84 are presented in table 3.2. All countries had a better conservation record in 1981–4 than in 1976–80; in eastern Europe up to 1980 consumption continued to grow considerably more rapidly than production. Over the whole period, only Romania and the GDR conserved energy at a rate similar to that of the major western countries.

This illustrates the general point that Soviet-type economies lack an automatic mechanism for adjusting to such an important relative price change; they can react only when the planners make the matter a sufficiently high priority. Although a price increase would cause households to switch their expenditure away from energy, it would have little effect on industrial users. Enterprises' planned level of costs would rise and planned profits fall to reflect the price increase. Since the increase would be built into the plan, the incentive to conserve energy would be scarcely any greater than before. It is only when the planners impose lower *physical plans* for energy consumption on enterprises that one can expect much progress in energy conservation.

Reforming the economic mechanism

It is precisely because the authorities were aware of the defects of the traditional, centralized system of planning developed under Stalin that considerable effort has been expended, over the last three decades, in devising ways to improve it. There is a fundamental difference, however, between those countries (Yugoslavia and Hungary) which have essentially given up the idea that the central planners should set out detailed physical targets for subordinate organizations, and those which have clung on to this system of planning by instruction. Since Hungary and Yugoslavia are discussed in later chapters, the concentration here is on the more limited type of reform. The discussion will focus on the Soviet Union, since this is the country for which the literature in English on the experience of reform is the most comprehensive, but the broad conclusions hold equally well for eastern Europe, even if the detail is different (see, for instance, Zielinski, 1973).

The first point is that reforms of any significance have a long gestation period. A proposal has first to be convincingly argued and accepted in principle by the political leadership. Then it is applied experimentally to a group of enterprises or a whole industry in a limited area (such as one of the Baltic republics). If this is a success, then its consequences and detailed application in various sectors of the economy have to be assessed, and the plan instructions and bonus systems adjusted accordingly. Finally, when the reform is officially announced, it is not applied immediately to all enterprises: on the contrary, it is usually some years before all units are converted to the new system. Thus, if we take the Soviet reforms that were announced in the autumn of 1965 (and treated with a great deal of fanfare), we find that the experimentation process began in 1962, and the reform was not projected to cover the whole of industry until the end of 1968, whilst completion for the service sector was not anticipated before the end of 1970. This delay gives some idea of the amount of bureaucratic effort involved in the whole process.

Part of the 1965 reform consisted simply of a reversal of Khrushchev's reorganization of the planning system, dismantling the regional economic councils established in 1957 and returning to a ministerial pattern. However this was accompanied by measures which were stated to be designed to replace 'administrative methods by economic levers' in the planning process. The number of plan indicators handed down as instructions to enterprises was reduced from 38–40 to 8–9, and the intention was that, instead of enterprises being instructed on every important issue from above, they would take some significant decisions themselves in response to the incentives offered to them by the bonus system. The reform made little difference to the behaviour of the central planners, who continued to construct materials balances and to devise plans for each ministry in the form of gross output. The change was confined to the lowest level of the planning hierarchy, the enterprise. This in itself was not conducive to a successful reform, because the enterprise was subordinate to a ministry which was primarily interested in gross output in value terms (the success criterion of the ministry's own plan), and if necessary the ministry would order the enterprise to bump up this indicator whatever the effect on enterprise profits and bonuses.

Two important aspects of the planning process at the enterprise level which remained substantially unaltered by the reform were investment and materials supply. Raw materials continued to be obtainable only against an allocation certificate from the planners; although it was said in 1965 that the aim was gradually to establish a wholesale trade in means of production, which would do away with the system of physical rationing, no significant step was ever taken in this direction. Investment decisions continued to be largely monopolized by the higher authorities, and to be financed out of the national budget, except that enterprises could now set up a development fund to finance small investments of their own. In an attempt to discourage wasteful use of capital, a 6 per cent rental charge was introduced on all capital financed from the state budget; however this was largely an accounting change, since residual profits were not retained by the enterprise and continued to go to the state.

The reform affected most the performance indicators for output and labour. For labour, the only plan indicator was to be the total wage bill; employment and wage rates were to be decided by the enterprise. Except for a few key products, physical output targets were abandoned and replaced by a target for sales revenue. The main object of this change was to discourage the production of unsaleable goods. Profitability became a more important consideration than before, because payments into the enterprise bonus fund (and also the development and social and cultural funds) were linked to it. Payments into each of these funds followed a complex formula, but were generally a function of profitability and sales revenue. This was intended to give managers an incentive to increase profitability, and for this reason it was deemed possible to drop cost reduction as a plan indicator.

In order to reduce misallocation of resources because of price distortions, a complete recalculation of prices was carried out, based on average production costs in 1964–5. The new price lists were brought into force in late 1966 in light industry and in mid-1967 in heavy industry. Nevertheless the bonus system contained some anomalies. For example, the rules for payments into incentive funds expressed payments as a proportion of the enterprise's wage and salary bill. This had the effect of penalizing reductions in labour costs relative to other methods of increasing profitability. On the whole, though, such anomalies were of relatively minor importance.

However, within a few years the attempt to replace administrative methods by economic levers was tacitly deemed a failure. This happened, despite the fact that many enterprises appeared to have responded with alacrity to the incentives offered and earned very large bonuses. What, then, were the problems? First, since all bonuses were based on fulfilment and overfulfilment of the plan, the new system rewarded most those enterprises which had built up hidden reserves of plan slackness, which the new system tempted them to mobilize. Such enterprises were being rewarded, not for greater achievement relative to others today, but for successfully hoodwinking the planners in the past. Secondly, the great reduction in compulsory plan indicators gave enterprises much more scope for manipulating the scheme to their own advantage. For instance, the elimination of costs as a compulsory indicator increased the tendency to concentrate on expensive products in order to boost sales revenue. This, again, was a result of the fact that the economic levers were all plan-related. Thirdly, the reform caused a marked divergence of wage rates between enterprises. Those with the greatest opportunity to shed labour could increase wage rates faster than others, and indeed an acceleration of money wages occurred. Moreover, there also seemed to be a tendency towards an incrase in the number of white-collar workers. Both these tendencies were regarded as undesirable by the planners.

The authorities expressed their discontent in a gradual restriction of the enterprise's scope for independent decision-making. A compulsory plan indicator for average wages was restored. Rules about the expenditure of incentive funds became increasingly tight, and in 1967 and 1968 only half of these funds were spent, probably because of difficulties in obtaining materials for unplanned investments. The reform was never officially declared dead; it was just quietly overrun by a creeping reimposition of central controls. Though experimentation and the search for an improved economic mechanism have continued, subsequent adjustments reveal no inclination to alter the system of addressing instructions to enterprises on all important matters. The experience of the 1960s reforms is regarded as proof that enterprises tend to misuse the freedoms that they are given, and that profit incentives and the planning system can coexist only under the most rigorous bureaucratic supervision. Accordingly the word 'reform' has been carefully avoided in later legislation.

In 1971, the interesting notion of counter-plans was introduced. Enterprises were invited to offer stiffer plan targets than those suggested by the ministry, and bonuses for fulfilment of this counter-plan were larger than those for overfulfilment of the original plan. On the other hand, if the counter-plan was not fulfilled, bonus calculations would be based on the original plan. Thus the scheme was devised in such a way that enterprises could not lose from undertaking a counter-plan. However this statement does not take into account the ratchet effect of planning from the achieved level. To offer a counter-plan would invite higher plan targets in subsequent periods. Probably because of this, the counter-plan idea has not caught on. In 1978 they were offered by only 17 per cent of industrial enterprises, and the average increase in output offered was only 0.25 per cent (Hanson, 1983); by 1981 only 7 per cent of industrial enterprises were offering counter-plans (Bornstein, 1985).

The most important single measure of the later Brezhnev years was the July 1979 Decree on the Improvement of Planning and the Economic Mechanism. This consolidated some changes already implemented, established a perspective for the 1980s, and also introduced some novelties. It authorized a further reform of industrial prices, to come into effect on 1 January 1982. Its provisions reflected the concern of the authorities with economy in the use of labour and materials, as these resources became increasingly scarce and expensive, and with raising the quality of output. The methods used illustrate the current perception that economic levers are best regarded as useful adjuncts to, rather than as substitutes for, administrative rules. Bonuses in manufacturing were to be made dependent chiefly on output quality, labour productivity and fulfilment of delivery contracts. Fulfilment of delivery contracts, to the tune of 98 per cent, became a necessary qualifying condition for a bonus after 1982. This idea was first tried in 1974, but its effective use was hampered for a time by the problem of the fair treatment of enterprises whose deliveries were incomplete because of shortages of supplies from others. The intention is to ensure that enterprises fulfil their customers' demands, but it is doubtful if most contracts are sufficiently detailed for this check to be really effective, and registering fulfilment of all delivery contracts is likely to be a substantial drain on administrative resources.

The problem of product quality was already being addressed in the mid-1970s, with the 1976–80 Five-Year Plan being described as a 'plan for quality'. A certification system was established whereby products were placed in three major quality categories, and if a product was placed in the highest category, the enterprise could apply for a price surcharge, the proceeds of which would boost its incentive fund. This measure has certainly had the effect of raising the proportion of highest-quality output in the total, from 6.5 per cent in 1976 to 15.5 per cent by 1982 (Bornstein, 1985). To what extent this improvement is real, rather than merely formal, is hard to say. The highest quality category (the 'state seal of quality') is supposed to meet full international standards, and is awarded by a commission to which the enterprise makes a case by comparing its product with chosen items from the catalogues of western producers. The commission consists of representatives of various state committees and of the producing and using ministries, but it is doubtful whether the commission really contains the expertise to make a critical judgement on the claim before it. A photograph in a catalogue is hardly a substitute for practical testing, and, of course, the enterprise has the advantage of selecting the catalogue.

Labour productivity was reintroduced as a plan indicator in 1973, and the 1979 Decree reinforced its significance as a determinant of bonuses, by allowing all above-plan savings on wages to go into incentive funds, and penalizing these funds for above-plan wage expenditures. In addition, social insurance taxes were raised sharply, in order to increase the cost of labour. A decree of July 1981 has established essentially the same pattern for raw materials. For the first time, materials expenditures are affecting bonuses, and the prices of a number of important materials have been substantially increased (Schroeder, 1982).

The most important single innovation introduced by the 1979 Decree, the replacement of gross by net output as a planning indicator, may also be interpreted as a materials-saving measure, since it was intended to remove the incentive to pad output by concentrating on items with a high raw material content (and hence a high price, because of the cost-plus pricing principle). Net output is not calculated by subtracting expenditures on inputs from gross output, but by the more complex procedure of establishing a 'net' price for each product (this is done by the State Committee on Prices) and multiplying it by the quantity, to produce what is known as normative net output. However, higher organizations are more interested in gross rather than net output, and thus continue to exert pressure on enterprises to pay attention to gross output measures.

Much effort in recent years has gone into finding ways to induce enterprises to reveal and release underutilized resources. The counter-planning idea seems to have been largely ineffective. The 1979 Decree restated the objective of making the Five-Year Plan an accurate forecast of future annual plans, which would reduce the role of planning from the achieved level, without providing any reasons why this should now be possible. The State Planning Commission has devoted much time to the calculation of norms of all kinds, especially for the usage of labour and materials, but also for other quantities such as profits and investment project completion times. The purpose of these norms is to provide a criterion for identifying areas of slack and inefficiency in the system.

What emerges from this brief survey is a sense that the authorities have become increasingly ingenious in devising improvements to the rules of the game, without being able to come to grips with the fundamental causes of dissatisfaction with the performance of the economy. Bonus systems have become immensely complex and differ from ministry to ministry in response to technical differences in the field of application. Because success in economic performance is a multi-dimensional entity, the regulations multiply and inevitably contain inconsistencies. Almost any alteration to meet one objective is found to have unfortunate effects elsewhere. Gertrude Schroeder has described this process as the treadmill of reforms. The published statistics do not suggest that tinkering with plan indicators and bonus schemes makes much difference to overall performance. Slight improvements can be made, priorities can be imposed, but the sluggish, conservative behaviour of enterprises is a reflection of the bureaucratic principles on which the economy is run, rather than the distortions introduced by any particular bonus system. It remains unclear how radical the new leadership in the Soviet Union is prepared to be in response to this. It has expressed interest in the Hungarian experiment and enlarged the scope for private enterprise, but other measures, such as tougher quality controls and a reorientation of investment priorities towards the modernization of machinery, seem more traditional.

In a sense the recent Soviet attempt to make bonuses dependent on contract fulfilment represents a recognition that in many respects the customer is a better judge of producer performance than the planner. Kornai (1959, 1980) has argued at some length that in a centrally planned economy, the tautness of markets makes a good deal of difference to producer-customer relations. If there is a generalized condition of shortage, customers have to accept what they can get, which is frequently not exactly what they want. They have to accept unsatisfactory quality and forced substitution. If market conditions favour the buyer, customers have much more scope for returning poor quality goods and getting producers to respond to their needs. Customers then have greater bargaining power when drawing up contracts with suppliers, so rules relating bonuses to contract fulfilment are more effective. If Kornai is right, a buyer's market would greatly improve the functioning of a socialist economy. But, as we shall see in the next chapter, centrally planned economies have a strong tendency towards a seller's market and a pervasive condition of shortage.

Notes

1 Storming by no means results just from interruptions to the production process during the plan period (although this is a significant factor). To an important degree it is deliberate enterprise policy. Since plans are not finalized until after the period to which they refer has begun, and ministries may continue to juggle plan targets between enterprises long after this, it is not advantageous for an enterprise to rush ahead in the early part of the plan period, for fear of attracting a stiffer plan.

4

Growth in the Centrally Planned Economy

Introduction

The discussion of the planning system in the last chapter was exclusively static. Nothing was said about investment or technical progress, which are matters of major concern to both the planners and the political leadership. The drive to overcome age-old Russian backwardness was one of the chief motivations behind the original attempts at planning in the 1920s and the 1930s. In this chapter this dynamic aspect of the centrally planned economy is considered first. Then the discussion moves on to a recent attempt to theorize the behaviour of the Soviet system, focusing on the notion of the *soft budget constraint* developed by János Kornai. Finally this chapter considers the evidence that these economies suffer from persistent excess demand, as Kornai suggests.

Investment

In the centrally planned economy, enterprises are *guardians* of a certain portion of social capital rather than its owners. Although the enterprise is a legal entity and is responsible for the plant and equipment which it possesses, it is entirely subordinate to the ministry and hence to the central planners. Enterprises may be allocated new capital, or have some of their existing stock removed, at the will of the higher authorities. At the extreme, enterprises may be disbanded and their assets dispersed to others. This means that an enterprise's formal responsibility for its capital equipment is not matched by the same financial stake in it that a capitalist firm has. In fact an appropriate analogy for a socialist enterprise under central planning is not so much with a private firm as with the bureaucrat's relationship to his or her desk and pen: these things have been allocated because they are necessary to perform the tasks set by superiors, and their cost is of no immediate interest to the user.

At the centre, the planners have the task of achieving a socially efficient rate and distribution of investment. They have to decide how many resources to devote to investment *in toto*, and to break this down by ministry, making allowance for any large projects transcending ministerial boundaries which they intend to fund separately. The ministries in their turn have to subdivide their investment allocation by enterprise. It has been clear ever since the late 1920s that this bureaucratic system of investment allocation has no difficulty in expending whatever funds are made available. The subordinate units make bids to their superiors, each seeking to prove that their investment project is better than their competitors', and the sum of these bids exceeds the allocated funds. Because it is the state's money which is being spent rather than the enterprise's own, and because enterprises can assume that if a project turns out to be loss-making, this will be compensated for in the profits target embodied in the plan, there is very little inherent risk attached to making investment project proposals. For the enterprise manager, expansion of the enterprise represents an effective promotion. Local party leaderships may also be active in agitating for investment in their area, for similar reasons. On the other hand, to fail to make a bid for investment resources would at best look like a lack of faith in oneself, and at worst a cavalier attitude to the great project of socialist construction. For all these reasons, enterprise managers find it advisable to bid for more investment funds than they are likely to receive, and the higher authorities find themselves having to cut down the bids.

In the Soviet Union and eastern Europe much intellectual effort has gone into the establishment of optimal criteria for choice between alternative investment projects. Like the decision to introduce rental or interest charges on capital, this is part of an attempt to ensure that investment resources are used efficiently. Without going into the matter, the methods used broadly resemble rate of return or present value criteria as used in the west, although of course they are complicated by distortions in the price system. The fact that land has no price, for instance, is likely to have meant that the agricultural value of a piece of land has not always been adequately taken into account in siting factories. Dyker (1983, p. 47) cites one such case relating to the high-grade cotton-growing area of Tadzhikistan. More generally, the drift of prices away from costs of production in between major price reforms, and the failure to resort to marginal cost pricing where marginal and average costs differ significantly (as in the raw materials and fuel sectors) are persistent sources of distortion.

Perhaps more important than this, however, is the evidence that the investment process under central planning can be grossly inefficient.

Two articles were published in the Soviet Union in the 1960s demonstrating that the gestation period of a sizeable sample of investments was 2–2½ times what was normal abroad, and there is no evidence of any improvement since. Although planned completion dates are often not demanding, 50 per cent of projects are not completed on time (Dyker, 1983, p. 36). A major reason for this is that subordinate units have every incentive to understate the cost of a project. If the costs are underestimated, the project looks more attractive on paper because its prospective rate of return is higher and it makes less of a hole in the investment budget. Enterprises know that once a project gets started the funds to complete it will eventually be forthcoming, whatever the cost overrun, because to complete an existing project is still cheaper than to start an entirely new one. The upshot of all this is that too many projects are authorized, ones which should have been completed are not, and the construction industry becomes hopelessly overstretched. According to three large samples of investment projects in the USSR in the period 1966–75, the typical project suffered a cost escalation of 30–40 per cent between design and implementation, and the number of projects under way at any one moment far exceeds the number which the construction industry could hope to complete on time (Dyker, 1983, p. 63).

It might be thought that the ministries would help the planners to counteract the tendency towards cost underestimation. Ministries might, for example, approve projects to the sum of only 70–80 per cent of the money available. However, the ministries are engaged in the same kind of bargaining game with the planners in order to push up their share of the investment cake. If their enterprises can show large numbers of projects with high prospective rates of return, ministries are only too glad to use this as a bargaining tool of their own. Thus, far from acting as the planners' policemen in the matter of cost underestimation, the ministries surreptitiously endorse the tactics of their subordinates.

The reform of 1965 in the USSR tried to counter these tendencies by (1) introducing interest charges on capital financed out of the state budget, and (2) providing more scope for decentralized investment, financed out of the enterprise's production development fund and not requiring prior approval from higher authorities. As mentioned in the last chapter, the first change had little effect, because enterprises are not residual claimants on profits anyway. The second was short-lived. The growth of decentralized investment was inhibited by the fact that it could be undertaken only after the plan was formulated, so that materials were often hard to obtain. After 1971, when the decentralized investment plan was for once overfulfilled by 26 per cent and the centralized investment plan underfulfilled by 4 per cent, the authorities began to exert increasing supervision over 'decentralized' investment, so that the differences between centralized and decentralized investment are now purely formal (Dyker, 1983, p. 31).

Since 1979, the objective of making ministries and enterprises self-financing has been formulated, and appears now to be receiving considerable emphasis. If achieved, this would mean that every economic unit would finance its own investment, and the hope is that it would treat the capital more as if it owned it. However it is extremely unlikely that such an objective can be achieved without radical changes to the whole system of economic management, because prices remain fixed for such long periods during which they inevitably diverge further and further from costs, so that some firms are bound to make losses whilst others make large profits. To revise prices more frequently would be a major administrative undertaking.

There is much concern in eastern Europe and the USSR over the pattern of investment. It has been claimed, for example, that (1) too much investment is now going into the exploitation of mineral resources in technically difficult areas of Siberia, when investment in conservation measures would show a significantly higher return; (2) the number of auxiliary workers per production worker is far higher in the USSR than in the west; and (3) the rate of modernization of equipment is far too low. These problems can be related to the position of the enterprise under central planning. They arise because the economic system does not give the enterprise the required signals and incentives. In capitalist economies, a rise in the price of a raw material stimulates firms to search for ways to conserve its use. If certain aspects of the firm's activities are much more labour-intensive than the rest, as real wages rise the incentive to find ways of saving labour in this area grows. Likewise, the profitability of old machinery is continuously reduced as real wages rise over time, and this in itself constitutes a signal that the machinery needs to be replaced: once operating costs are equal to the value of output, it is more profitable to scrap the machine than to operate it.

Under central planning, things are not so simple. There *is* an incentive for the enterprise to reduce costs and increase profits, other things being equal, because this tends to raise bonuses. But the benefits may be only transient because of the effects of planning from the achieved level. The enterprise is likely to find that in the next period its contributions to the state budget have been increased. Thus there may well be ways in which enterprises could significantly reduce materials consumption per unit of output, if they made the effort to investigate the possibilities; but these possibilities tend not to be explored whilst present plan allocations of materials continue and profits plans incorporate the costs involved.

The incentive to scrap equipment is undermined by the desire to hoard labour. If the enterprise finds it preferable to accept a certain amount of surplus labour in order to facilitate plan fulfilment, despite the extra costs involved, then the opportunity cost of labour is zero. Therefore it becomes profitable to go on using an old machine even if its operating costs exceed the value of its output. The enterprise will of course put in bids for new equipment, but it will hope that it will be allocated *new labour* to operate it; there is no incentive for it to *volunteer* to transfer labour from old equipment (unless there are special rewards for this). Hence the existence of pockets of inefficient labour usage is not signalled to the planners, who find that, because of their ignorance, it is hard to force enterprises to disgorge surplus labour by appropriate reductions in plan allocations.

The high proportion of auxiliary workers is a little more difficult to explain. No doubt it reflects, in part, the convenience of 'repair and maintenance workers' (and also on-the-job training schemes) as a label for hoarding labour, and also the self-supply of spare parts. But there is a tendency for some auxiliary operations, such as loading and unloading, to remain highly labour-intensive, whilst production itself has become highly capital-intensive. This may reflect the lack of incentive for enterprises to apply for investments that are transparently labour-saving, because the higher authorities may capture all the gains by reducing the enterprise's employment allocation. Because of this effect, the system has a built-in bias towards extensive investments, which enlarge the enterprise's claims on inputs as well as its outputs, as against intensive ones, which would obtain more outputs from the same inputs: this will be discussed further in connection with technical progress.

These problems are not unknown to the planners, but they are not necessarily the most pressing ones. As a result, matters tend to drift until they reach some sort of crisis point, when the planners decide to accord the problem a priority which brings results. In the 1970s, labour productivity became an important plan indicator because the planners were worried by the prospect of serious labour shortages. In the 1980s the exhaustion of cheaper and geographically convenient sources of raw materials has caused them to build systematic cuts in materials usage into plans. Very recently, awareness of the bias towards extensive investment has given rise to a drive to modernize the USSR's stock of machinery. But whilst these issues become priorities, others necessarily suffer from neglect.

Technical progress

It is well known that the Soviet Union and eastern Europe have sought to import western technology on a considerable scale. This was part of the development strategy in the 1920s, and became significant again in the 1970s. In the period from 1948 to 1970 technology imports were inhibited by east-west political tensions, as they have been to some extent also since 1980, though the balance of payments difficulties of eastern Europe were probably a more important factor at this time. Of course there is nothing unnatural in eastern European countries being technological importers from the west, given that they are on a lower level of development. The real issue is the capacity of their own economic systems to generate and diffuse technical innovations.

Eastern Europe began to export manufactures to the west before 1970, but has done much less well in this respect than some other newly industrializing countries, and the general assessment is that east European products have not been able to compete effectively on quality. Winiecki (1986) quotes some figures indicating that value per kilogram of exports to the west has declined over time, suggesting a deterioration in quality relative to competing products. Students of the technical level of Soviet industry have concluded that the Soviet technological lag is not being reduced (Amann et al., 1977), despite the relatively high growth rates officially recorded.

In terms of technological effort, as measured by the number of persons engaged in research and development (R&D), the USSR seems to rank at least as high as any country in the west. R&D personnel and the science budget expanded very rapidly in the 1960s, and total R&D manpower may have been as much as 50 per cent greater than the US by 1966 (Zaleski et al., 1969, p. 503). In terms of output of research papers, though, the USSR lags behind the US. Basic research is organized through the Academy of Sciences, and applied research is concentrated in institutes operated by ministries, though some takes place in the laboratories of higher education establishments. There were about 1700 applied research institutes in the USSR in 1969 (Berliner, 1976, p. 39). There is thus an organizational separation between the research institute and the enterprise that has no counterpart in capitalist countries, where the bulk of industrial research is carried on in companies' own research departments.

The evidence suggests that this separation leads to inefficiency. Since the bulk of R&D work is financed by the ministry (though since 1962 a certain proportion is covered by direct contracts with enterprises), the ultimate utility of an innovation is rather less important than satisfaction of the higher bureaucracy, and this has often led to much superficiality and even duplication in research. In contract research, the client enterprise is obliged to pay even in the event of a 'negative result', so here too the pressure on the R&D organization to produce positive results is limited. Moreover, even a successful and useful innovation has a long way to go between development and implementation. The innovation has first to be approved by a committee, such as the State Committee on Inventions and Discoveries, as desirable and useful. Then it goes off to an engineering design organization for detailed specification of manufacturing techniques and materials. After this work has been approved by a further committee, a construction–engineering organization is involved if the innovation requires any new construction. Finally an enterprise agrees to produce a prototype. All this happens at the leisurely pace which befits a bureaucratic organization (Berliner, 1976, p. 102).

Quite apart from any effects on the speed of implementation of innovations, the separation of users and R&D organizations may well inhibit the identification of possible improvements. In the west, it is common for an accumulation of small improvements to be as significant in technical progress as major breakthroughs, and the concentration of R&D in manufacturing firms encourages contact between user and researcher and the swift exploitation of such opportunities. In the USSR, the contract system is supposed to enable enterprises which identify possible improvements to bring in an R&D organization to investigate them. However the incentive for an enterprise to act in this way is not so clear, and it may well have good reasons for choosing to ignore the possibility. Not only does the enterprise have to foot the bill for the research, but it has to consider the headaches created by any changes in material inputs and technology which the innovation involves, in an institutional setting where it faces no obvious penalty if it does nothing. In a centrally planned economy characterized by persistent shortages, limited information available to the centre, and a ratchet effect in plan formulation, the risks involved in exploring possible innovations are more obvious to the enterprise than the rewards. The ratchet effect of planning from the achieved level will tend to cream off the rewards from the enterprise itself to society as a whole, whilst the risks are greater than in a market economy if any alteration in supplies is involved, because the existing stock of supply relationships, in which the enterprise has invested heavily, will be devalued – an important consideration in an economy characterized by widespread shortages. The one form of innovation which the system encourages is that designed to overcome supply bottlenecks. Gomulka (1986, chapter 3) quotes two Polish studies which indicate that a substantial proportion of innovations are of this type. The problem is that from a social viewpoint such innovations are often regressive, increasing enterprise flexibility at the expense of overall economic efficiency.

The planners attempt to combat this conservatism by blanket use of norms and steady reductions in planned use of inputs per unit of output. This is a powerful weapon, but an indiscriminate one: it produces the result that enterprises hoard potential improvements to the production process, over and above what is required to fulfil the current plan, in order to slacken next period's plan for cost reductions.

For product as opposed to process innovations, it has long been recognized that the traditional emphasis on gross output above all other considerations was discouraging, because teething problems associated with the production of new items would make plan fulfilment more difficult. In 1957 the system of managerial bonus payments in the USSR was adjusted to give credit for new products. More recently, the emphasis has been transferred to product quality rather than product innovation *per se*, and bonuses have been related to the proportion of output in the various quality categories described in the last chapter.

More broadly, since 1946 there has been a system of special payments to individuals or groups deemed responsible for significant innovations, though these payments remain small compared with what an independent innovator can earn from a patent in the west.

The general picture which emerges from this is that if, as is usually the case, the bonus system is not geared primarily towards stimulating innovation and the plan deadlines are relatively short, enterprises are likely to resist innovation until it is forced on them by the higher authorities through stiffer plan requirements. This is because, in order to insure themselves against interruptions of supply of raw materials and spare parts, they have made a substantial investment in existing supply relationships and in getting to understand and being able to produce replacement parts for existing machinery. Any investment which involves new machinery or new materials devalues the existing painfully accumulated stock of knowledge. Thus, when enterprises make bids for new investment, they concentrate on proposals for extensions of capacity which offer grounds for obtaining larger quantities of labour and material inputs as well. Such projects help to enlarge the factory, without disrupting its existing mode of operation.

One proposed method of combating such conservatism is to stabilize future plan targets, as the USSR is attempting to do by setting targets for each year of a five-year plan at the beginning of the quinquennium, and basing bonuses on these pre-set annual targets. This is portrayed by its proponents as the answer to the negative effects of planning from the achieved level, though it seems more likely just to transfer them to a longer timescale. Whilst stable targets would imply that enterprises could reap the benefits of an innovation made early in the quinquennium for a full five years, the corollary of this is that the temptation to postpone innovations in the fourth and fifth years would be very strong. The fact that successful hoarding of innovations could produce slack plans for a full five years lays this proposal open to the usual charge against enlarging the scope for enterprises to make their own decisions: that they are rewarded more for their past success in hoodwinking the planners than for any genuine social contribution. However, so far this is pure hypothesis: the system is still a long way from stabilizing Five-Year Plans.

Since planners have virtually no detailed information about the innovation possibilities available to enterprises, they are forced to resort to blanket measures, imposing economies through lower plan allocations of inputs and rewarding productivity increases with bonuses. Such methods are liable to produce a rather linear form of development, precluding major structural changes. This probably explains why the socialist countries have largely failed to replace steel by plastics, as noted in the last chapter.

Just as important as the rate of implementation of a technical innovation in a single enterprise is its rate of diffusion throughout the industry. This is where a socialist economy might seem to have a decisive advantage. Whereas in a capitalist economy firms actively try to prevent their competitors from getting hold of their innovations, in a socialist economy technical knowledge is public and indeed technologically advanced enterprises are expected to open their doors and to encourage others to learn from them. Empirical studies of the rate of diffusion of new technology in the Soviet Union reveal the opposite picture: if anything, the rate of diffusion is slower than in the west (Amann et al., 1977). Since the system contains no intrinsic incentive for an enterprise to imitate others' inventions, diffusion has to be imposed through the bureaucratic mechanisms of the planning process. In practice this appears to be slower than the competitive mechanisms of a market economy (the long gestation period of investments must also pay a role here).

Thus the overall picture created by more detailed microeconomic analysis of technical progress in a centrally planned socialist economy complements the impression given by the macroeconomic data in chapter 2. There are many points of resistance and obstacles to innovation, which have their roots in the pervasive bureaucratization of economic life and the conservatism of enterprises whose incentives are entirely plan-related. The burden of economic progress then falls on those who formulate the plan, but these are professional administrators without direct experience of current research and development work or of technical problems and opportunities at enterprise level. Their response is to fall back on general principles, in recognition of their own lack of information. The relevant information exists only within the basic units to which the plan is addressed, but these units have an incentive to disguise their capacities in innovation just as much as in current production. The authorities are then forced to compensate for these inefficiencies by devoting as many resources as possible to investment and R&D, for otherwise they cannot provide a politically acceptable rate of growth of consumption.

An interesting question is raised by the existence of certain relatively advanced sectors of the Soviet economy, such as military and space activities. Are conditions in these sectors more conducive to technical progress and customer satisfaction than in the rest of the economy? It was mentioned in chapter 1 that the whole system of central planning evolved primarily because it permitted the ruthless imposition of priorities, in particular, in the 1930s, to squeeze consumption in order to release resources for investment. Today, favoured sectors continue to get priority treatment, particularly in matters of materials supply. There is an official name in the USSR for special projects which fall into this category: they are called 'objects of the central committee'. There are three possible ways in which priority sectors might have an advantage over the rest of the economy.

1 The customer is able to exert much closer control over the producer, because the political leadership regards the satisfaction of that customer's needs as a priority. The decisive influence is the customer rather than the producing enterprise's ministry.

2 Research and development can be integrated more closely with production. Again, this is because the customer, who has direct experience of the use of the products, can influence the direction of research and supervise product quality in a way which the planning system does not normally permit.

3 The enterprises in this sector do not have difficulty in obtaining materials of the required quality or spare parts for machinery, because other ministries will order their enterprises to treat them as priority customers and will expect their needs to be met even if the order is not covered by the enterprise plan.

It is also true that the sectors usually regarded as superior in performance are ones in which the cost of production is often a secondary consideration to product quality: in Berliner's terminology (1976, p. 506), they tend to be 'mission-oriented' rather than 'economic' activities. I doubt whether in itself this is a factor of great significance; for the reasons cited above, a priority sector would probably be able to function rather better than the rest of the economy even if the customer attached great importance to cheapness, because the decisive factor is the influence and political backing which the customer has. Indeed it is often said of Soviet military equipment that it reveals a preference for reliability and robustness over technical sophistication.

Of course it goes without saying that the advantages conferred on priority sectors work to the disadvantage of the rest of the economy, whose requirements are pushed down the queue. By definition there can only be a few priorities at any one time.

The soft budget constraint

The Hungarian economist János Kornai has made a major contribution to the theory of the centrally planned economy by introducing the concept of the soft budget constraint. A soft budget constraint means that an enterprise is not held responsible for the financial consequences of its decisions: its losses will somehow be covered from somewhere. The softness of the constraint relates not to the fact that enterprises are permitted to make losses and be subsidised *per se*, but rather to the open-endedness of this commitment. If an enterprise is given a specified sum as a subsidy and told that if it fails to make a profit after the subsidy has been taken into account, it will be closed down, that is a hard budget constraint. If the enterprise is given to understand that any loss will be subsidized, however large, the budget constraint is soft. In the former case the enterprise will be under pressure to keep its loss below a certain minimum; in the latter it will not. This is an idea which had appeared in economics previously only in the rather unsatisfactory form of 'returns to bargaining with governments'. This expression is misleading in suggesting that there are calculable costs and rates of return involved, and that the government subsidies are determined *ex ante*, whereas the whole point of the soft budget constraint is that nothing is determined *ex ante*; the government simply picks up the bill *ex post*.

Kornai argues that in the traditional system of central planning, the enterprise in a socialist economy faces a budget constraint which is rather soft, and certainly much softer than is normally the case in capitalist economies. This may seem surprising, since an emphasis on cost control dates back to the earliest days of NEP. The planning system has always included cost targets, and at some periods fulfilment of cost plans has been an important determinant of managerial bonuses. But this has not always been the case. Throughout the Stalin period gross output was the overriding target, and this was clearly reflected in the bonus system. Moreover costs have never been more important than output; at best they have had equal significance.

However the bonus system is not the essential point; the real question is the plan-relatedness of performance indicators, which results in pressure for slack plans from subordinate units. Subordinate units claim as many resources as possible, and once these allocations have been written into the plan, it is scarcely possible to penalize anyone for using them. Even if the bonus system emphasises profitability, the plan base for profits will reflect the materials allocations that have been obtained. If the enterprise succeeds in obtaining a generous allocation of materials, this will raise costs and reduce profitability, but since it has the same effect on the planned values of these indicators, the enterprise is not penalized. The absolute profitability of the enterprise is of little consequence, since everyone knows that the price system contains many irrationalities which will cause some enterprises to be loss-makers and some extremely profitable through no fault of their own. Loss-making enterprises are not in fact penalized; their losses are simply covered by transfer of funds from profitable enterprises. Although a law has existed in the Soviet Union since 1954 allowing enterprises to be declared bankrupt and their assets sold off, there is no known instance of this law having been applied.

This aspect of the economic system has a powerful political foundation which rests on the desire to give the workforce a security which it never had under capitalism. Kornai (1980, p. 315) expresses this very well:

> Anxieties about failure of the firm disappear; neither managers nor workers need be afraid of bankruptcy. Not only is employment guaranteed, but even the actual place of work. The state functions as a universal insurance company which almost fully compensates every loss, even if occasionally only after some bargaining.

As part of this social contract, incomes are fully insured against the fluctuations of the market. A drop in exports is not immediately felt by the workers producing them; rather, the firm is compensated. But this commitment to socialist principles of income distribution quickly expands into a generalized tolerance of inefficiency and waste. With the removal of insecurity, the pressures to be forward-looking, imaginative and responsive to new developments also disappear.

The same tendency to make claims for resources irrespective of financial consequences exists in the field of investment. If an enterprise is not penalized for making a loss then it will not be penalized for unprofitable investment either. As a result, although profitability may influence the types of investment for which the enterprise makes claims and the projects which the higher authorities prefer, the thought that an investment may be unprofitable does not in itself prevent a claim being made.

The knowledge that not all claims can be met itself encourages the inclusion of projects which are not expected to be authorized. This 'investment hunger' displayed by lower-level organizations in the planning hierarchy has its roots, according to Kornai, in the job identification of managers, that is in their desire to improve the units under their authority, although there is also career motivation: a larger, more important enterprise improves the standing of the managers. With a soft budget constraint, these pressures towards high investment are not restrained by financial considerations.

In sum, subordinate units in the planning hierarchy are as profligate with resources as their superiors allow, and consciously adjust their behaviour in order to maximize the resources made available in the plan. There are at least three ways in which budget constraints are soft: (1) all measures of financial performance are plan-related, so unnecessary claims on resources which are ratified by the plan never incur any financial penalty. (2) Since profitability is only one of a number of plan indicators, the bonus system does not necessarily penalize management greatly for below-plan profit performance, if the plan is fulfilled in other respects. (3) Unprofitable investments are not penalized, because profits plans are adjusted accordingly.

Thus the softness of the budget constraint has several dimensions, but centres around the limited and often purely superficial importance of profit and loss accounting.

Kornai makes an explicit link between the softness of the budget constraint and the tendency of the economic system towards excess demand, which by creating shortages reinforces the propensity to hoard resources, because otherwise production is constantly threatened by the non-availability of some vital input. But for investment hunger to result in excess demand, it must be ratified by the higher authorities: there must be pressures in the system which prevent the investment allocators from rationing claims strictly enough. Since project cost underestimation is commonly of the order of 30 per cent, as much as 25 per cent of investment funds would have to remain unallocated to counteract it. In practice the contingency reserve is seldom more than a few per cent, and urgent projects are almost invariably discovered to absorb it. This behaviour on the part of the planners reflects the attitudes of the political leadership. As has been abundantly clear since the time of Stalin, the interests of the leadership point systematically in the direction of maximizing the rate of investment; the one-party political system makes them largely immune from the wrath of consumers, and consumption tends to be regarded as a cost necessary to maintain the quiescence of the population rather than as an end in itself. Thus the planners find it advisable to allocate their investment budget, knowing that it will create excess demand, but passing the blame if asked onto the claimants who underestimate the costs of their projects.

The planners make considerable efforts to prevent excess demand in the sphere of investment goods from spilling over into the consumer goods sector, where shortages are politically damaging. Their chief instrument for achieving this is to ensure that wage and salary payments do not exceed planned amounts, the demand from which is expected to be met by planned supply at prevailing prices. The separation of the monetary system, according to which cash can be drawn only for payments to labour and other enterprise expenditures must be made by cheque, greatly eases the task of policing this aspect of the plan, which is usually one of the most precisely fulfilled (Adam, 1976; Kornai, 1980, p. 377). Nevertheless, the planners' success in this respect is not a sufficient condition for balancing the consumer goods market, as this depends on supply also. Thus excess demand for consumer goods can develop because the output plan is not fulfilled. This may occur for many reasons: economy-wide underfulfilment of the plan, adverse weather conditions in agriculture, failure to complete on time factories whose expected output was included in the plan, reduced imports due to unexpected balance of payments difficulties, and so forth. The extent to which consumer goods markets in centrally planned economies have in fact been characterized by excess demand is discussed in the next section.

The difference between the investment and the consumption goods markets arises from the fact that consumers face hard budget constraints. Wage payments are rigidly policed and consumer credit is much less developed than in capitalist countries. Because of this, excess demand for consumption goods can quite easily be soaked up by price increases, as occurred in the Soviet Union in 1935 and 1947, though more recently there has been great reluctance to resort to this because of its political unpopularity. Upward revisions of wholesale prices have been more frequent, but the softness of enterprise budget constraints makes these revisions much less effective in relieving shortages. Generally, the price rise is built into enterprise cost plans, so buyers are fully compensated.

To what extent have the reforms discussed in chapter 3 altered the softness of budget constraints? A greater stress on profitability does not in itself indicate a hardening of budget constraints, if incentives continue to be plan-related. The decentralization of investment decisions was probably the most significant aspect of the reforms as far as enterprise budget constraints were concerned: one might expect firms to take more care of funds over which they had more control. In so far as enterprises could take investment decisions on the assumption that plan targets would be unaffected (because the investment did not require detailed justification to the higher authorities) the resulting investments might reflect profitability considerations more than centralized investment. On the other hand, freed from supervision by higher authorities, decentralized investment might accentuate the tendency towards self-supply, since such investment directly relieves bottlenecks which threaten plan fulfilment. The shadow cost of an input to the enterprise is not at all the same thing as its accounting cost. If an input (e.g. labour) is in surplus in the plan and there are no difficulties in obtaining the amounts allocated, its shadow cost is effectively zero; whereas if the allocation of steel is taut and deliveries are unreliable, its shadow cost is far above the price. This explains why so many spare parts are produced by the users. For genuinely decentralized investment, therefore, the budget constraint is harder but the private shadow costs are distorted and largely outside the knowledge of the planners. The return to a centralized system of investment allocation suggests that this was not regarded as an improvement over the traditional system.

More recently, the USSR has proclaimed the objective of introducing self-financing for ministries and enterprises. It is undoubtedly the intention of the proponents of this move to harden budget constraints, by forcing ministries and enterprises to find the finance for their own investment. In this way, it is hoped, they will cease to regard investment funds as a free good. In reality it is difficult to imagine the principle of self-financing being instituted in other than a purely formal way under the present economic system. Taken literally, it would mean that a loss-making ministry would be refused investment credits even though its customers may be complaining loudly about shortages of its products. This is hard to envisage. The most likely outcome, if the principle were taken seriously, would be that the investment would be authorized without overtly contravening the principle: that is, either the ministry's product price would be raised or its contributions to the state budget reduced. Either way, the softness of budget constraints would reappear. Every manager would get the message that if the investment can be presented as sufficiently urgent, the finance for it will be found.

The tendency to excess demand

It has long been said that Soviet-type economies, unlike most market economies, tend towards a state of excess demand or, as it is sometimes known, 'repressed inflation'. This latter expression implies that, if prices were not fixed administratively, they would rise. Strictly, what is involved is a repressed price increase and not necessarily a repressed inflation. Whether or not the price increase would stop once the initial excess demand had been absorbed, or whether forces would come into play that would lead to continuous inflation, is a question which cannot be answered merely from the observation that prices at a given moment are below market-clearing levels. For this reason the term 'excess demand' is more accurate than 'repressed inflation'.

It is quite evident that during much of the Stalin period the Soviet economy experienced considerable excess demand. Consumer goods prices were below market-clearing values for most of the period from 1927 to 1947. In the period of the First Five-Year Plan, not only did agricultural output fall, but expenditure on wages ran far ahead of plan. Although price increases in the mid-1930s more or less brought the consumer goods market back into balance, excess demand reappeared after 1937, and was of course considerably exacerbated by the war. The question is whether, since 1947, the normal state of affairs in the USSR and eastern Europe has been one of excess demand.

There seems to be little disagreement that this has been the case in the investment goods sector, for the reasons described in the previous section: investment hunger, cost underestimation and the desire for growth on the part of the political leaders. For the consumer market the evidence is less clear-cut. The planners make considerable efforts to balance this market, although not necessarily with success. They do have the option of allocating conservative wage plans as an insurance against shortfalls in supply, but they are under continual pressure from subordinate units to increase labour allocations. On top of this there is the political desire for taut plans, which derives not just from directly political concerns but also from a widespread feeling that the economic system is like a mule which has to be continually beaten in order to get results. Optimistic plans are a means of driving the economy to higher levels of performance.

> In plan targets, party authorities pay much attention to the 'mobilising effect'. The idea is that the targets should be high enough so that, to meet them, enterprise managers will be forced to utilise reserves in the expenditure of inputs and organisation of production. This is not to say that party leaders want to promote unrealistic plans, but . . . they do not trust management as a whole. Planners are to construct plans on the principle that targets should be higher than managers would set themselves. (Kushnirsky, 1982, pp. 84–5)

If half of the function of the plan is to mobilize production possibilities that are merely suspected to be there, the argument that any particular target looks infeasible loses much of its force. Genuine complaints about unrealistic plans face the objection that targets cannot be allowed to encourage shirking by producers. The author of the above passage cites an incident from his own experience where the head of the Light Industry Department of the Ukrainian Planning Commission lost his job for insisting on what he considered to be a realistic plan target instead of a higher one.

It seems that the tradition of taut planning inherited from Stalin has persisted in the Soviet Union, but one should hesitate before concluding that taut planning is an inevitable law of the centrally planned economy. Even in the USSR plan targets appear to have become steadily more modest and realistic over time. Granick (1975) formed the clear impression from managers that plan targets in Romania were attainable and put much less strain on enterprises than in the USSR. In the GDR in the 1960s more emphasis seems to have been put on technological improvements and the development of new products than on the growth of output, although a greater degree of tautness crept in after 1970 (Keren, 1973).

Casual observation also suggests that the Soviet Union should not be taken as typical. The phenomenon of queuing seems to be more prevalent there than in eastern Europe. Queuing does not in itself signify excess demand; it can occur either because retail outlets are insufficient in number or slow in operation, or because particular goods are in short supply whilst stocks of others remain plentiful. Indeed both of these factors operate in socialist countries. The elimination of petty capitalism in eastern Europe from 1948 to 1950 caused a large drop in the number of retail shops which has never been made good. Pryor (1977) found that a significantly lower proportion of the labour force was engaged in retail trade in socialist countries than in capitalist countries at a similar level of development. In addition, the incentive to sell is not present to any significant degree, and concern about theft inhibits the development of self-service (Turcan, 1977). Nevertheless, if under-capacity in retailing were the sole cause of queuing, the problems would be over once the customer reached the counter, whereas the normal experience in centrally planned economies is that many goods are out of stock. Because prices are fixed and plans are made a year in advance and cannot adjust quickly to shifts in consumer demand, the supply of consumer goods cannot be matched to the demand for individual commodities, even in a state of macroeconomic equilibrium where value of supply equals the value of demand. The buyer is constantly required to engage in what Kornai calls 'forced substitution' (of a good that is available for the one that was originally wanted). The 'deficit goods' will then be out of stock whilst the 'surplus goods' fill the shelves.

In these circumstances consumer behaviour will be conditioned by the prevalence of shortage even if from a macroeconomic point of view the consumer market is in equilibrium. Forced savings will appear to the extent that consumers are unwilling to spend their money on the goods that are readily available. Thus the existence of forced savings does not in itself prove that the consumer goods market is in a state of macroeconomic, as opposed to merely microeconomic, disequilibrium. This makes it difficult to judge whether there is in fact significant macroeconomic disequilibrium. For the USSR, it seems fairly certain that the 1970s were a period of accumulating excess demand in consumer goods markets. Agricultural output fell far short of plan, and the ratio of the free collective farm market prices to the fixed state prices steadily increased. After the reform of 1965, wage payments tended to outstrip the supply of consumer goods (Nove, 1982, p. 380). At the same time the volume of personal savings bank deposits grew very rapidly. A rise in accumulated savings is to be expected in a community with rising real incomes and a poorly developed system of consumer credit, but the speed of the increase strongly suggests a state of excess demand.

Portes and Winter (1980) have attempted to test the hypothesis of excess demand in consumer goods markets for the four most advanced east European countries (the GDR, Poland, Czechoslovakia and Hungary) over the period 1955–75. They develop simple models of supply and demand, and derive estimates of the degree of excess supply or demand for each year by comparison of the demand and supply quantities generated by the model. The conclusion they reach is that these countries have not been in a state of continuous excess demand in consumption goods markets. The GDR is estimated to have experienced excess demand in all but four years, but for the other countries excess supply appears as frequently as excess demand.

This sort of test is sensitive to model specification and the results do not always conform to the impressions of informed observers at the time. A more complex model for Poland developed by Quandt et al. (1987), involving plan data and incorporating planners' reactions to shortage signals, finds excess demand in 1959, 1961, 1968 and 1971–5, compared with Portes and Winter's 1955–6, 1958–9 and 1971–3. For the GDR, the Portes and Winter results do not confirm the impressions of Keren (1973) that plans were slack in the mid-1960s. For Hungary, Portes and Winter estimate strong excess supply in 1965–7 and 1971–2, and they do not confirm Portes's earlier view (1977) of excess demand in 1974–5 and excess supply in 1969.

Some east European economists have criticized this disequilibrium theoretic approach on the grounds that shortage is endemic (Winiecki,

1985; Kornai, 1982). The main thrust of these criticisms seems to be against the question posed rather than the methods used to answer it. If people already face shortages of many goods, it is no consolation to them if the value of unsold goods on the shelves is equal to what they would like to spend on the commodities which are not on offer. To this extent, the aggregate balance of the consumer goods market is irrelevant to the consumer's experience and behaviour. Excess demand exacerbates a condition of shortage which already exists; it does not qualitatively change it.

One way to express this would be to say that shortage is a multidimensional concept which in disequilibrium macroeconomics is reduced to one dimension, because the models assume only one consumption good. From a technical point of view, this simplification may well introduce bias into the empirical results, by omitting forced substitution. Because 'surplus goods' remain available even in situations of aggregate excess demand, demand factors will still influence the observed level of consumption, and this may bias upwards the estimated market equilibrium position (Bleaney, 1987). Thus, although there seems to be agreement that consumption goods markets in centrally planned economies are often in a state of excess demand, the frequency of occurrence of states of excess supply is still very much open to debate, and will probably remain so for some time to come.

5

Poland: the System in Crisis

Introduction

Poland deserves a chapter of its own, not because of any special characteristics of its economic mechanism, but because its recent history has been dominated by a socio-political crisis more profound than any other in post-war eastern Europe, in which the conduct of macroeconomic policy during the 1970s played a central part. Starting in late 1970, popular opposition steadily deprived the regime of its freedom of manoeuvre in vital economic matters, and pushed the party leadership into a reckless dash for growth which, in other political circumstances, would probably have been rejected as too risky. By 1975 the edifice was starting to crumble, and a new wave of strikes against government policy in June 1976 left the leadership virtually helpless. This episode effectively set off the downward spiral leading to the crisis of 1980–81.

The origins of these developments can be traced back, with hindsight, as far as 1956. That year marked the first of a series of victories by the popular movement over the leadership of the Polish United Workers' Party (PUWP). As mentioned in chapter 2, riots in Poznań at the end of June 1956 led to attacks on public buildings, and 54 people died in the disturbances. These events were at first condemned as counter-revolutionary agitation, but within days the line changed and the legitimacy of grievances against the political and economic 'errors' of the Stalin period was admitted. Those convicted of involvement in the riot received lenient treatment. The old Stalinist leader, Bolesław Bierut, had conveniently died in March, and the Poznań events gave the reformists in the party the upper hand. A policy of 'democratization' was announced, raising public expectations, and the split between reformist and orthodox elements in the PUWP became increasingly public through the summer. In October the Central Committee met to elect a new leadership. The orthodox faction had warned the USSR that 'counter-revolution' was on the ascendant in Poland, and in an attempt to influence events a group of Soviet leaders, including Khrushchev, made an unannounced appearance at the meeting, whilst Soviet troops made menacing manoeuvres around Warsaw. This crude intervention had no immediate result, for the reformists carried the day and Władysław Gomułka, who had been purged from his post as General Secretary of the PUWP in 1948, was re-elected First Secretary, delivering a withering attack on Polish Stalinism. Gomułka acquired enormous prestige in the country for having stood up to Khrushchev's pressure, although the Soviet delegation had no doubt been able to satisfy itself of something that was only to become fully clear to the Polish population over the next two years: that Gomułka was much more orthodox than his rhetoric of 1956 suggested.

The Gomułka years

The apparent willingness to contemplate genuine reforms (together with the awful warning of Hungary in November) enabled the new Polish leadership to keep control of a volatile political situation, but not without considerable concessions. The goal of collectivization of the peasantry was effectively abandoned, just as the rest of eastern Europe was planning to complete the process. Real wages, which had fallen by about seven per cent from 1950 to 1953, were allowed to rise by 43 per cent between 1953 and 1957 (Brus, 1986, Table 24.10; similar changes occurred in Hungary and Czechoslovakia). Fundamental reforms of the economic system were discussed at the highest level. In 1956 enterprises received only eight obligatory plan targets, an all-time low, and the general tenor of the reform discussion was towards quite radical decentralization. A law was passed establishing directly elected workers' councils with considerable formal authority. Peasants were permitted to leave the collective farms.

Over the next two years Gomułka steadily chipped away at these gains, reimposing orthodoxy in all areas except agriculture (where he had already been an opponent of collectivization in 1948). By 1958 the workers' councils had lost their independent status and were once more controlled by the PUWP. The economic reform discussion was siphoned off into an Economic Council whose recommendations were accepted only in a very much watered-down form (for a discussion see Brus, 1986, pp. 97–104), and the number of obligatory indicators transmitted to enterprises rose steadily to reach 19 by 1959 (Zielinski, 1973, p. 116). Enterprise independence was further undermined by the creation of industrial associations in 1958. Gomułka mended his fences with Khrushchev in October 1957, thereby sacrificing much of his former

Table 5.1 Changes in real wages in Poland 1947–70 (per cent)

Period	*Plan*	*Actual*
1947–9	–	58
1950–5	40	4
1956–60	30	29
1961–5	22.5	8
1966–70	10	10

Sources: Zielinski (1973), Table 1.10
Fallenbuchl (1977), p. 819

popularity in Poland. From 1959 the investment tempo was raised, a year later than elsewhere in eastern Europe, and real wages growth was kept below 2 per cent per annum right through to 1970. As table 5.1 shows, the squeeze on consumption was increasingly built into plans, and if one allows for the omission from the official price data of hidden inflation of 1–2 per cent per annum (see chapter 7), then real wages scarcely grew at all between 1958 and 1970, which was an important factor underlying the explosion of discontent over the food price increases of December 1970.

For Poland the 1960s were a decade of disillusion; after the dashing of the hopes raised by 1956, there seemed to be little of interest to discuss, although the cultural atmosphere remained more liberal than in most of the rest of the Soviet bloc. Gomułka's leadership lacked inspiration and any real sense of direction, and factionalism began to develop within the PUWP. The 'partisan' faction of General Moczar, which played on nationalist, anti-Semitic and anti-intellectual sentiments, brought matters to a head with a full-scale ideological offensive in 1968, and at the Party Congress in November of that year Gomułka required the fulsome support of Brezhnev to check Moczar's advance.

In 1969 some new economic reform proposals were announced for implementation on 1 January 1971. These included a reform of producer prices and a complex incentive scheme which linked the permitted growth of enterprise wage funds to performance. The details of this were published in 1970, and envisaged a total rise in the wage bill of not more than 16 per cent up to 1975. Thus it was made clear that the policy of austerity for consumers would continue, whilst the incentive scheme created considerable uncertainty about future wage movements in any particular enterprise. The secret part of these proposals consisted of a planned readjustment of retail prices, raising them for some foods in order to reduce government subsidies and alleviate shortages, and reducing them on some manufactured goods. In order to eliminate panic buying, the public was given no inkling of these changes, which were introduced overnight on Saturday 12 December 1970, less than a week after the signing of the Warsaw Treaty in which West Germany finally recognised Poland's western borders. The price of television sets and refrigerators was reduced, but many food prices were increased: flour by 16 per cent, sugar by 14 per cent and meat by 17 per cent (Ascherson, 1981).

This action set off immediate and massive protests. On Monday 14 December, shipyard workers in Gdańsk downed tools and marched on the town's PUWP headquarters. On Tuesday a general strike was declared in Gdańsk, and the unrest spread to Gdynia and other towns. In Gdańsk, the police opened fire on the demonstrators (on Gomułka's orders) and people were killed. The workers responded with occupation of the shipyards and factories. By Thursday the disorder had spread to Szczecin and the Council of Ministers decided to declare a state of emergency. No concessions were offered. On Friday some Politburo members opposed to the policy of repression without compromise demanded a meeting to discuss the situation. Under pressure, Gomułka suffered a slight stroke and went to hospital. This opened the way for his removal from the leadership, though at the Politburo meeting on Saturday it still took seven hours to secure a majority for this. Edward Gierek, an ex-coalminer, was elected First Secretary, and on Sunday 20 December appeared on television, acknowledging the leadership's mistakes and promising a revision of economic and other policies. The strikes were then called off (Pelczynski, in Bromke and Strong, 1973).

Gierek made no immediate concessions; his promises of change remained vague until, in February 1971, a renewal of the strike movement forced him to rescind the price increases (the price reductions were retained) and to scrap the new incentive system. Reform remained on the agenda, but the PUWP now set itself the task of re-establishing its credibility by raising living standards. According to official figures real wages increased by 5.6 per cent in 1971 and by 6.4 per cent in 1972. The volume of imports increased by 13.8 per cent in 1971 and by 22.1 per cent in 1972, with finished consumption goods taking a slightly higher share of these imports than in the late 1960s. The situation of private farmers was improved by an increase in prices paid for their products (especially for meat), reductions in taxes, the elimination of obligatory deliveries after 1 January 1972 and their inclusion in the national health scheme. A more relaxed attitude towards the independent peasant was also signalled by an increase in the proportion of land acquired by the State Land Fund which was allowed to return to private use. With the

Table 5.2 Polish goods imports from developed capitalist countries 1970–5

Year	*As % total goods imports*	*As % goods exports to DCCs*
1970	26	92
1971	27	95
1972	34	121
1973	44	159
1974	51	177
1975	49	190

Source: Fallenbuchl (1977), Table XIII

help of good harvests, the real income of the agricultural population increased by 15 per cent in each of the years 1971 and 1972 (Fallenbuchl, 1977; Brus, 1982).

Gierek's gamble

In the wake of the December events the as yet unpublished Five-Year Plan for 1971–5 was abrogated and a new one, involving higher consumption targets, was formally approved by the Sejm (Parliament) in June 1972. This envisaged a slight acceleration of NMP growth to 7 per cent per annum (compared with 6 per cent per annum in 1966–70), and average annual increases in real wages and real per capita incomes of 3.4 and 6.7 per cent per annum respectively – much less than had in fact been occurring in 1971–2, and thus appearing to presage a dramatic deceleration in the growth of living standards in 1973–5, on the pattern of 1958–60. But Gierek had staked his political reputation on a permanent improvement in economic performance, and moreover he knew that because of the history of the Gomułka era, the population would react sensitively to any sign of a return to austerity. Besides, the above-plan growth of output in 1971 and 1972 gave grounds for optimism. Meanwhile the scope for borrowing in hard currency from western banks had increased with the progress of *détente*, the West German ratification of the Polish frontiers and the current state of monetary ease in the west. Even under Gomułka, the notion of importing western technology had been gaining currency. Now it suddenly seemed that borrowing from the west could give Poland the modern equipment that would put it on a permanently raised consumption path. So from the middle of 1972 onwards vast amounts of machinery and equipment began to be imported from the hard-currency area. Table 5.2 shows how imports from the west grew from just over a quarter to a half of all imports in just four

Table 5.3 The economic development of Poland 1970–5

	% change over previous year					
	1970	*1971*	*1972*	*1973*	*1974*	*1975*
Net material product	5.2	8.1	10.6	10.8	10.5	9.0
Gross industrial output	8.1	7.9	10.7	11.2	11.4	10.9
Gross agricultural output	2.2	3.6	8.4	7.3	1.6	−2.1
of which animal products	−1.1	6.6	9.0	8.2	4.2	−1.0
Net material product used	5.0	9.8	12.5	14.3	12.0	9.5
Gross fixed investment	4.0	7.4	23.0	25.4	22.3	10.7
Consumer prices	−0.2	–	2.6	6.8	3.0	4.7
Real wage	1.7	5.6	6.4	8.7	6.5	8.8
Trade balance with market economies ($ million)	110	84	−256	−1116	−1849	−2411

Source: UNECE (1985/6, 1986/7), Appendix Tables

years. By this time they were approaching double the value of exports to the same area, although in 1970 and 1971 Polish visible trade with this area had been in surplus. Whilst imports overall continued to be dominated by raw materials, imports of finished goods, which had been split more or less equally between consumption and investment goods in 1971, were divided almost 2:1 in favour of the latter by 1974.

At first this policy of modernization by foreign borrowing seemed to accomplish all that was expected of it. Some relevant statistics for the 1971–5 period are presented in table 5.3. Between 1972 and 1974 investment was increasing at more than 20 per cent per annum. Growth of net material product accelerated to 9.8 per cent per annum, despite relatively weak agricultural performance, and the improvement was exclusively due to faster labour productivity growth, with no contribution from additional growth in employment. Moreover, in contrast to the general trend in eastern Europe, capital productivity continued to improve (see table 2.6). Far from stagnating after 1972, real wages actually increased still faster, according to the official figures. These results generated an atmosphere of euphoria at the Seventh PUWP Congress in December 1975.

Nevertheless this pattern of growth was clearly not sustainable. A wide and steadily increasing trade deficit with the convertible currency area had opened up; by 1975 the burden of debt service had reached 26 per cent of export receipts and the large trade deficit put the debt burden on a strong upward trend. Export prospects had deteriorated as western markets moved into an era of slower growth. With the exception of this last point, this situation could have been foreseen when the new economic policy was initiated in 1972. But the political leaders chose to believe that the gap could be closed by a big expansion of exports to the west from the new production facilities that had been installed with western credits and machinery. No account was taken of, or attempt made to limit, the possible dependence of the new plants on imported inputs, nor was it considered whether these exports would be able to hold their place in international markets over time rather than be outstripped by new technical developments as time passed.

A further difficulty requiring urgent correction was a growing imbalance in consumer goods markets. In both 1974 and 1975 net agricultural output had fallen quite sharply, partly because of unfavourable weather conditions, but also probably because of a more hostile official attitude towards the private sector. At the same time demand for higher quality foods rose extremely fast, because of rapid increases in real incomes combined with a falling relative price. After February 1971 the government had initially committed itself to a temporary freeze on food prices, but this commitment had been repeatedly extended at a time when prices of manufactured consumer goods were rising noticeably. Between 1970 and 1975 per capita consumption of meat rose by 30 per cent, and food subsidies reached such a level that peasants increasingly found it profitable to sell milk to the government and purchase dairy products at subsidized prices in the shops rather than make them at home, as before.

In recognition of these problems, the plan for 1976–80 envisaged a halt to the investment drive and a much slower growth of consumption, whilst the deficit on the balance of payments was projected to be closed by 1979. Although the extent of the country's foreign debt was not disclosed by the government at this stage, the publication of the 1976–80 plan guidelines in late 1975 made the population aware of the deterioration in economic prospects. The government also kept secret its intention to end the freeze on food prices in an effort to cut the fast-rising burden of food subsidies.

Avoiding the sensitive Christmas period, the government selected what it thought was a favourable moment to raise prices in June 1976. The rises were far greater than in December 1970, in recognition of the accumulated distortion caused by the prolonged price freeze. The price of meat was to rise by an average of 69 per cent, of sugar by nearly 100 per cent and of dairy products by over a third. This was met by a country-wide stoppage of work the next morning, and within twenty-four hours the proposed increases were withdrawn.

The rapidity and comprehensiveness of this retreat demonstrated the weakness of the government's position. Its tactics had been unfortunate.

Table 5.4 The economic development of Poland 1976–80

	% change over previous year					*Average*	*Average*
	1976	*1977*	*1978*	*1979*	*1980*	*1971–5*	*1976–80*
NMP	6.8	5.0	3.0	−2.3	−6.0	9.8	1.2
Gross industrial output	9.3	6.9	4.9	2.7	–	10.4	4.7
Gross agricultural output	5.0	−7.2	5.4	−3.7	−15.2	3.7	−3.5
NMP used	6.5	2.2	0.5	−3.7	−6.0	11.6	−0.2
Gross fixed investment	1.0	3.1	2.1	−7.9	−12.3	17.5	−3.0
Consumer prices	4.7	4.9	8.7	6.7	9.1	3.4	6.8
Real wage	4.3	−2.4	−2.2	2.1	4.0	7.2	1.1
Trade balance with market economies ($ million)	−2022	−1293	−1395	−1175	−1232	−1110	−1423

Source: UNECE (1985/6, 1986/7), Appendix Tables

By failing to raise food prices more gradually earlier and then deciding to keep the increase secret, it had deprived itself of the possibility of preparing the public for it, and a subsequent opinion poll showed that fully a quarter of the population was unaware that food was subsidized, at a time when the subsidy bill was approaching 8 per cent of national income (Mason, 1985, pp. 48–9). Thus the reaction was not altogether surprising, given the scale of the increases.

From this moment on the situation became increasingly difficult for the government. Its own rhetoric, and the policies of the previous five years, had raised expectations of growth in living standards to new heights just at a time when such expectations could not possibly be met because of the need to close the gap in the balance of payments. After 1976 the volume of imports ceased to rise, and economic growth began to grind to a halt. After 1978 NMP began to fall quite sharply, partly as a result of difficulties in agriculture, but in 1980 even industrial output was falling (table 5.4). Because of the diversion of resources to correct the balance of payments, NMP *used* was no greater in 1980 than in 1975. Inflation became significant, and when allowance is made for an element of hidden inflation it is unlikely that real wages were still increasing. (Askanas and Laski (1985) estimate an average rate of hidden inflation over the period 1964–78 of 2.3 per cent per annum, but their calculations using 1973 data suggest a rate of only 0.8 per cent per annum for 1964–73, and 5 per cent per annum for 1973–8. If the latter figure is correct, average real wages were actually falling in every year from 1976 to 1979). A further indication of the squeeze on consumers is the fact that from 1976 onwards savings deposits grew more slowly than money incomes (UNECE, 1984/5, Table 4.5.9), an unusual situation in eastern Europe (though some part was played in this by Poland's relatively high inflation rate eroding the value of past savings).

At the same time the government's defeat in June 1976 stimulated opposition activity which it no longer felt strong enough to suppress decisively. Most significant of the opposition groups was the Committee for the Defence of Workers' Rights (KOR), formed by a group of intellectuals originally in support of workers charged in connection with the 1976 events. Its formation signalled an alliance of intellectuals and workers which had been conspicuously absent in 1970, and also at the time of the suppression of the students' movement in 1968, and was to be of great significance in subsequent developments.

The formation of Solidarity

On the pressing matter of food prices the government now trod very gingerly indeed. It set up commercial shops where meat could be bought without queuing at roughly twice the normal price, but even by mid-1980 less than 10 per cent of meat was being sold in this way. In 1979 and 1980 the economic situation began to deteriorate very markedly. On 1 July 1980 the government announced that another 2 per cent of meat sales, including bacon, would go through the commercial outlets, although local authorities were instructed to apply this measure with circumspection. The announcement resulted in immediate stoppages of work in a number of places, in support of demands for a compensating wage rise. The government instructed managers to concede, but this only encouraged the movement to spread and the pay demands to escalate over the ensuing weeks. KOR set itself up as an information centre for the workers' movement, yet the government failed to take decisive action against it. On 14 August workers at the Gdańsk shipyards came out on strike, and put the demand for a free trade union at the top of their list, making it clear in negotiations with government representatives over the next few days that this was a non-negotiable demand (Ascherson, 1981).

These events prompted a government reshuffle in which Gierek, though temporarily retaining the post of First Secretary of the PUWP, lost effective power to Stanisław Kania, who formally deposed him on 6 September (Ash, 1983). Kania's line continued to be one of appeasement and concession. The Gdańsk Agreement ending the strikes, signed on 31 August by representatives of the government and the shipyard workers, recognized the right to form independent trade unions and the right to strike. This was an historic step, though on the government's insistence these new unions would continue to acknowledge the 'leading role' of the PUWP. By mid-September, when the name 'Solidarity' was formally accepted at a national delegates' meeting of the new union, it already claimed three million members. By the end of the year the number was close to ten million. When the question of legal registration came up, the leaders of Solidarity resisted more strongly the inclusion of a clause recognizing the leading role of the party, and the government ultimately had to be content with the addition of the relevant passage of the Gdańsk Agreement as an appendage to the union's statutes, whilst the clause was omitted from the statutes themselves.

This question of recognizing the leading role of the party encapsulated the dilemma facing Solidarity. It could not ignore the 'geo-political reality' facing Poland, that is that the country was a member of the Soviet bloc, the essentials of whose political system would be preserved by force if necessary, as in Hungary in 1956 and Czechoslovakia in 1968. Far from recognizing the leading role of the PUWP, the very existence of Solidarity expressed the profound distrust of the population in it, and the desire to exercise some permanent power of veto over its policies. Yet the natural extension of the movement into the political arena was blocked by fear of Soviet intervention. It was a 'self-limiting revolution' that attempted to cram 'a radical wave of protest and class war into a "trade union" formula' (Staniszkis, 1984, p. 17). Precisely because Solidarity was the one institution not controlled by the PUWP, it became the focus for all expressions of discontent. At the same time its leaders were well aware of its anomalous and insecure position within eastern Europe, and that its existence was scarcely tolerable to the government on a permanent basis. To sustain their independence, Solidarity's leaders needed a movement permanently mobilized behind them. At first this was no problem, but as the months passed, Solidarity's difficulty in finding an effective strategy or role for itself within the existing system became increasingly apparent. Meanwhile, the economy's slide downhill became a headlong rush in the course of 1981. Solidarity had begun by pushing trade union demands such as wage increases and the end of Saturday working, which was conceded by the government (except for one Saturday per month) on 31 January 1981. But once it had become clear that the government lacked the authority to do anything to solve the economic crisis without the support of Solidarity, then the movement was pushed into an awkward position, in which it could not avoid some degree of joint responsibility for the situation.

Jadwiga Staniszkis has labelled this the 'identity crisis' of Solidarity, and dates it from April to July 1981. As can be seen from tables 5.4 and 5.5, the government had already acted to protect living standards to a

Table 5.5 The economic development of Poland 1981–6

	% change over previous year						Average
	1981	*1982*	*1983*	*1984*	*1985*	*1986*	*1981–6*
NMP	−12.0	−5.5	6.0	5.6	3.4	5	0.2
Gross industrial output	−10.8	−2.1	6.4	5.2	4.5	4.4	1.1
Gross agricultural output	3.8	−2.8	3.3	5.7	0.7	5.0	2.6
NMP used	−10.5	−10.5	5.6	5.0	3.8	5	−0.5
Gross fixed investment	−22.3	−12.1	9.4	11.4	6.0	3.0	−1.6
Consumer prices	24.4	101.5	23.0	15.7	14.4	18.0	29.9
Real wage	2.4	−24.9	1.2	0.5	3.9		−4.1*
Trade balance with market economies ($ million)	−865	−3	262	778	598	622	232

* 1981–5
Source: UNECE (1985/6, 1986/7), Appendix Tables

considerable degree from the effects of the crisis, allowing investment and exports to fall much more sharply than consumption, so by mid-1981 it had few economic concessions left to offer. No recovery programme could avoid substantial sacrifices for the population. As a trade union, Solidarity could hardly accept this. As a social movement, it could only do so if it could exchange an austerity programme for genuine participation in economic decision-making.

Thus in this period, the self-limiting revolution was forced to confront directly the issue of power. The government showed no signs of being willing to relinquish power to any significant degree. But in the spring of 1981 it seemed as if the PUWP itself might be radicalized from below. Many party members had joined Solidarity, most sympathized with its aims, and pressure for a greater degree of internal democracy was considerable. A significant exodus from the party began. In April 1981 it was announced that an Extraordinary Congress would be held in July, and the leadership was forced to concede the principle of election by secret ballot, in place of the usual rubber-stamping of names picked from above. But the discontent of the lower echelons of the party was directed more at the apparatus than at the political line of the leadership. This was reflected in the voting at the Congress itself. Only 8 per cent of the old Central Committee, and four out of sixteen members of the old Politburo, were elected to the new Central Committee. But when the new CC met to elect a new Politburo, all of Kania's nominees were successful against opponents nominated from the floor. Thus the discontent with the apparatus emerged, but the existing *leadership* was confirmed, and was able to consolidate its position. By contrast, the grassroots organization of the PUWP showed increasing signs of ineffectiveness and even disintegration (Mason, 1985, chapter 6; Sanford, 1984).

Having secured its rear within the party, the leadership prepared to settle accounts with Solidarity. It was even less inclined to offer any real power-sharing than before, whilst in Solidarity mounting frustration at the situation and the apparent impotence of the government stimulated an increasing politicization of the movement. The government media played on this as proof of the seditious character of the organization. The military began to exercise a higher profile. In February 1981 General Jaruzelski had been appointed Prime Minister; in October he replaced Kania as First Secretary of the PUWP. Shortly afterwards, 'military operational groups' were sent into the countryside 'to assist local government administrators in improving food supplies and enforcing law and order' (Ash, 1983, p. 237). Finally, on 13 December Jaruzelski announced that a state of war had been declared and power was now in the hands of a Military Council of National Salvation. The leaders of Solidarity were arrested, and all telephone communications cut. Enterprises were placed under the supervision of military commissioners. No mention was made of the PUWP, nor of Jaruzelski's position as leader of it; the party was effectively sidelined in a military coup. The success of the operation reflected its careful preparation, the trust of the population in the army and an increasing inclination through the autumn to blame Solidarity in addition to the government for the crisis, as opinion polls show (Mason, 1985).

Table 5.5 summarizes the performance of the economy since 1981. In 1982 output bottomed out and exports recovered, whilst imports continued to be cut back sharply. In February 1982 prices of food, heating and electricity were greatly increased; over the year as a whole consumer prices doubled, and real wages fell by a quarter. The authorities were able to contain protests organized in the spring by the now illegal Solidarity without great difficulty, and in July 1983 martial law was lifted. Over the next three years the government continued to squeeze consumption in favour of investment and the balance of payments, and output began to recover, but at a rate which suggests that the economic losses of the period of political crisis are permanent. In 1986 NMP was only 93 per cent of the 1978 level, and the plan target of less than 4 per cent per annum growth for 1986–90 is modest.

The balance of trade with the hard currency area has been in significant surplus since 1983, and the foreign debt, whilst still large and of

Table 5.6 Net convertible currency debt of Poland 1981–6

	1981	*1982*	*1983*	*1984*	*1985*	*1986*
Net debt (end-year, $ billion)	25.4	25.2	25.2	25.3	27.7	29.5
As % visible exports to market economies	446	460	436	431	496	521
Net interest payments on debt:						
As % of visible exports to market economies	51.0	55.5	52.1	46.0	44.7	43.2
As % of visible and invisible exports to market economies	38.2	50.9	42.1	36.4	32.5	30.8

Source: UNECE (1986/7), Tables 5.3.5, 5.3.6, 5.3.7

considerably greater significance than in any other east European country, is no longer careering out of control (table 5.6).

It is striking that the inflation rate has continued to be high. This has probably been facilitated by the package of economic reforms passed by the Sejm in July 1981, and at least partially initiated in 1982. These reforms are in theory the most far-reaching in the Soviet bloc outside Hungary, and envisage considerable decentralization of decision-making, although at first they were not consistently implemented and have probably made little difference so far to the overall functioning of the economy (Gomulka and Rostowski, 1984). It is likely that at the moment the authorities are not unwilling to see enterprises raising prices and wages regularly under the guise of reform, because this helps to disguise relative price movements and to prevent the return of the fetishism of constant food prices. In late 1987 the government announced its intention to push forward the reform process, but it clearly faced opposition from within, and at the time of writing it remains unclear what exact changes might occur.

Conclusions

What can we learn about the functioning of Soviet-type economies from the Polish experience? Perhaps the most striking aspect is the correlation between economic policy and the political situation. Up to 1970 the Polish pattern was not very different from that of a number of other east European countries, with real wages falling in the early 1950s, growing strongly in the period of de-Stalinization from 1953 to 1957, and then much more slowly as the investment ratio was gradually raised again. But the successful revolt of December 1970 set Poland on a different course. As in 1956 popular pressure resulted in a change in the leadership (which might not have occurred but for Gomułka's illness) and considerable concessions to consumers. Then in 1972 the new leadership began to succumb to the temptation of foreign borrowing on a grand scale. It is doubtful if it would have done so but for the political pressures created by the December events: the decision is a little reminiscent of Stalin's rush into collectivization in 1929, a big gamble by a government boxed into an awkward political corner. Foreign borrowing prolonged the consumer boom until 1975, and fuelled an investment boom as well.

By then corrective measures were urgently required, but in June 1976 the workers again forced the government to retreat ignominiously from a food price increase. After this episode, the government's political credibility and economic freedom of manoeuvre were reduced virtually to nil. Under the impact of enforced curtailment of imports, the economy sank into decline, and in August 1980 more government action on meat prices stimulated a wave of strikes, followed by the formation of the independent trade union Solidarity, thus precipitating a political crisis which lasted until the imposition of martial law in December 1981. Only after this were the authorities able to depress real wages and get the balance of payments deficit under control. This resolved the immediate political crisis but still left the country facing up to the consequences of the short-sighted policies of the Gierek era. In 1986 output was only at the same level as in 1976, and the foreign debt was higher in relation to hard currency export earnings.

The economic prospects therefore continue to look bleak even some years after the crisis of 1980–81. General Jaruzelski's inclinations are reformist, and by keeping the 1981 economic reforms on the statute book he has revealed his strategy as essentially Kádárist: to offer economic reform in place of the blocked political changes. However he faces a situation which is much less favourable both economically and politically than Hungary in the years after 1956. Economic stagnation and a huge weight of foreign debt make it virtually impossible to increase living standards at more than a modest rate. This was graphically illustrated by the referendum of December 1987, which solicited support for extensive economic and political reforms but also asked the population to accept sacrifices in the immediate future (it was known that these would include increases averaging 40 per cent in the price of food, housing and energy). The government failed to get the necessary 50 per cent of 'yes' votes from the electorate to either question.

The essential difference between Poland in 1980–81 and Hungary in 1956 is that in Poland the political crisis was much deeper and more prolonged; in Hungary the party lost control for only a relatively short period. This difference can be seen, amongst other things, in the way the ghost of Solidarity hangs over the whole of political life, and in the sluggish pace at which the party is being rebuilt. Moreover, Jaruzelski is compromised by his past in a way in which Kádár was not. Kádár was a purge victim, and was able to gain credit for his repudiation of Stalinist methods. Furthermore he did not actually plot the suppression of the popular movement, which was carried out by Soviet troops. Jaruzelski, on the other hand, was a member of the Politburo throughout the 1970s, and himself directed the whole government strategy against Solidarity, culminating in a meticulously organized takeover by the armed forces. For all of these reasons, the population is much more deeply alienated from the government, and the political gains from a strategy of economic reform are likely to be much more modest.

The history of the political crisis itself, from August 1980 to December 1981, is a dramatic illustration of the inability of the Soviet type of political system to tolerate any kind of challenge to the political monopoly of the party. The economic situation made it impossible for the government to offer material concessions that would be acceptable to Solidarity, and mere personnel changes had long since lost credibility. Yet to offer Solidarity power-sharing in matters of economic policy in return for austerity measures would be to confer legitimacy on a rival political authority in the country. The potential consequences of this would be unthinkable. Thus it was inevitable that the government would temporize until the movement became exhausted, and then act to suppress it.

Had the Soviet Union not loomed in the background, the crisis would certainly have led to the overthrow of the existing political system. Thus the ultimate lesson of the Polish events is the extent of the economic cost of maintaining such a political system in the face of the clearly expressed opposition of the population. A decade of economic growth has been sacrificed, and will never be regained.

6

Hungary: the Reform Model

Introduction

Hungary is worthy of special attention amongst east European countries because of its consistent commitment to a more decentralized form of planning than prevails elsewhere in the Soviet bloc. Whereas elsewhere 'reform' is a word which the authorities have been increasingly reluctant to use (because in most cases they no longer expect radical improvements from any changes to the economic mechanism which they are willing to contemplate), in Hungary the reform programme first implemented in 1968 has substantial political momentum behind it. The sensation that the country is exploring new and interesting paths in its economic life has become a major aspect of the regime's strategy for gaining political support, or at least acceptance. Hungary prides itself on being different, less dogmatic, and in vital respects more responsive and subtle in its attitude to economic questions than the rest of eastern Europe. One might also mention that the scope for free discussion, especially but not only of economic matters, tends to be greater: for example the journal *Acta Oeconomica*, published in English and Russian, contains many critical articles which one could scarcely imagine being printed anywhere else in the Soviet bloc, except in the most unusual circumstances.

The aftermath of 1956

To anyone observing the state of Hungary at the end of 1956 this would no doubt seem surprising. In early November of that year popular discontent that was swiftly taking on an overtly anti-Communist character had been suppressed by a Soviet invasion. The build-up to the crisis had strong similarities to that in Poland very shortly before, with the important difference that the Hungarian Stalinists clung to power longer and more effectively. When, on 23 October, the Central Committee finally turned to the reformist Imre Nagy in the face of massive street demonstrations, it simultaneously appealed to the Soviet garrison to help restore order in Budapest. This undermined Nagy's position as a reformist and demonstrated the government's weakness. Nagy got the Soviet troops withdrawn, but the popular movement, instead of subsiding and giving him the benefit of the doubt, developed faster than ever, focusing on demands for free elections and the withdrawal of Soviet troops. Nagy was more sympathetic to these demands than Gomułka, who knew where a line had to be drawn. On 30 October Nagy announced the return to a multi-party system; a few days later, under severe pressure, he stated that Hungary would withdraw from the Warsaw Pact. This was too much for the Soviet Union, whose troops moved in on 4 November. Nagy took refuge in the Yugoslav embassy. János Kádár, a purge victim of the early 1950s who had been appointed party leader on 24 October, took over the government.

Kádár was to remain in control for the next thirty years. Initially his policy was necessarily repressive and orthodox. The political police was reconstituted. Institutions that had grown out of the 1956 upheavals, such as the workers' councils, were swiftly emasculated and then suppressed. Moreover Kádár had to take account of the recrudescence of Stalinist ideas in the international communist movement at this time, as reflected in the strong condemnation of revisionism at the international communist conference of 1957, the renewed ideological polemics with Yugoslavia in 1958, and the drive to complete the collectivization programme and push up investment rates. Kádár was forced to go along with this, and to accept the execution of Nagy in June 1958 (Since December 1956 Nagy had been imprisoned in Romania).

In this atmosphere it was scarcely possible to proceed very far down the road to economic reform, although the government did give some indications of its willingness to move in this direction. For example, compulsory deliveries of agricultural commodities were completely eliminated, and in late 1956 a large committee of experts was set up to investigate the economic mechanism and make proposals for change. Although the committee's report, published in late 1957, was met by a long silence followed by strongly negative comments from the government, with hindsight it can be seen to contain most of the central elements of the later reform process: a relatively positive attitude to private sector agriculture, an important degree of price flexibility and decentralization of decision-making, and a concern that world prices should be accurately reflected in the domestic market, so that planners and enterprises made investments that were rational from the point of view of Hungary's international situation. This last point reflected the singular inappropriateness to Hungary of the Soviet model of development slavishly imitated by the country's Stalinist leaders. In marked contrast to the USSR, Hungary was a small country (population approximately ten million) poorly endowed with mineral resources. The drive towards autarky and the swift development of heavy industry in the early 1950s had created severe balance of payments difficulties, because the raw materials had to be imported, whilst agriculture, the only sector which could realistically pay for these imports, had been severely neglected. As a development strategy, this did not seem to be rational, and failed to recognize that small countries need to accept some degree of specialization in their industrial structure.

The period from 1957 to about 1965 might be described as a period of political consolidation, in which the economic mechanism was adjusted in small ways, but no major change was instituted. In 1957 a bonus fund was introduced for all workers, related to increases in enterprise profits, which could pay out annual amounts not exceeding one month's wage. A reform of producer prices, intended to bring them more into line with costs, was carried out in 1959. Greater emphasis was placed on sales as opposed to output as a plan indicator, and a capital charge of 5 per cent on all enterprise assets was introduced at the beginning of 1964. On the other hand, as in Poland, the marked reduction in compulsory plan indicators issued from the centre, which had occurred in 1956, was swiftly reversed (Brus, 1986). In the early 1960s there was a marked reduction in the number of industrial enterprises, through amalgamations, from 1368 in 1961 to 840 in 1965, and a number of trusts were formed, unifying formerly independent enterprises (Marer, 1986). Although some additional decision-making powers were devolved to large units thus created, this essentially represented administrative decentralization rather than the replacement of bureaucratic methods by economic levers. The motivation behind this reorganization was similar to that which elsewhere in eastern Europe and the USSR was leading to the creation of industrial associations, though a UNECE study (quoted by Brus, 1986, p. 107) did record the impression that supervision of enterprises was less detailed in Hungary.

If Hungary stood out in the early 1960s, it was largely for the political achievements of the government in gaining the grudging acceptance of the population, though its agricultural policy was also noteworthy. Kádár was able to rebuild the party (which had virtually disintegrated in 1956) fairly swiftly. The international situation also began to swing back in favour of reform, with the Twenty-second CPSU Congress in October 1961 giving the green light to a new wave of de-Stalinization. In an article in *Pravda* in December of that year Kádár wrote that 'despotism is not a socialist phenomenon' and launched his famous slogan, 'he who is not against us is for us'. In line with this dictum, in the early 1960s growing numbers of non-Communists were appointed to high state positions, and there was a noticeable liberalisation in cultural life (Fejtö, 1971).

In agriculture, the start of the new collectivization campaign was delayed until the end of 1958. Once begun, the campaign took much the same course as elsewhere, but in Hungary it was distinguished by a rather relaxed attitude towards private production. Collective farmers received some compensation for land and means of production contributed to the collective, and the household plots and animal stocks permitted were larger than elsewhere in eastern Europe. Over 50 per cent of collective farmers' income was derived from private production in the years 1960–5 (Brus, 1986). There was also substantial state investment in agriculture, and a steady improvement in prices paid for agricultural output. Kulaks were admitted into the collectives after 1962. The effect of these policies could be seen in the figures for agricultural output, which performed significantly better during the collectivization process than anywhere else in eastern Europe (Marer, 1986). In the decade to 1965 peasant incomes increased significantly faster than real wages. In short, the Hungarian government displayed a willingness to depart from the norm in its agrarian policy at quite an early stage. At the ideological level this was confirmed in 1967 by the official rejection of the traditional view that collective farms represented a lower form of socialization than state enterprises.

The New Economic Mechanism

It was in December 1964 that the party decided to move towards a more comprehensive economic reform, first details of which became public in November 1965. However, several months before that experimentation had begun in the agricultural sector. Collective farms were no longer to receive instructions from above about what to produce (with the important exception of bread grains); instead they would make production decisions on the basis of contracts signed with buying enterprises. At the same time the financial position of collective farms was improved by the cancellation of many of their debts, and a variety of welfare measures was extended to collective farmers. These moves foreshadowed the main principle behind what was to become known officially as the New Economic Mechanism (NEM): that detailed directive planning should be replaced by much greater freedom of enterprise decision-making about output.

At the time that the reform was being formulated, the leadership faced quite a difficult political situation because of the unexpected fall of Khrushchev in October 1964. Khrushchev had given Kádár strong support against the dogmatists in the Hungarian party, and the more cautious and conservative stance of the new Soviet leadership encouraged Kádár's opponents to launch an offensive against the reform measures, which probably met quite substantial opposition at the May 1966 Central Committee Plenum where the final shape of the measures was decided (Robinson, 1973). The continuing presence of this dogmatist element renders more understandable the backsliding which occurred in the difficult conditions of the early 1970s.

It was decided that the NEM would come into force on 1 January 1968. The delay reflected a recognition that the reform needed to be carefully prepared and treated as a consistent whole. During 1966 and 1967 working parties were established to study and make recommendations on all sorts of issues. From the start the intention was that the new system would have a logic different from the old one.

The most important change, and one that strikingly differentiated the NEM from reform measures elsewhere in eastern Europe (though there was a precedent in Yugoslavia), was the abolition of obligatory plan indicators covering current inputs and outputs. The central planners were to confine their attention to macroeconomic planning, regulating the economy through monetary and fiscal policy instruments, which would create incentives for enterprises to respond in the desired fashion. For the enterprise, instructions from above about current production were replaced by contracts with customers and suppliers. At the same time, physical rationing of raw materials and intermediate goods was largely abolished (this measure had been declared an ultimate objective of the 1965 Soviet reforms but never implemented). Enterprises were expected to maximize profits, and were given an incentive to do so through the bonus fund (distributed to managers and employees as bonuses) and the development fund (to finance additional investment), both of which were linked to profitability according to prescribed rules.

These measures were accompanied by a far-reaching reform of the price system. All producer prices were revised so as to bring them more into line with costs. A uniform exchange rate was introduced for all transactions in convertible currencies (to replace the previous system of differentiated rates) and the state monopoly of foreign trade was abolished, a number of enterprises now being permitted to initiate some foreign transactions on their own account. Administrative control of prices was considerably relaxed: whilst some goods continued to have fixed prices, for others only a maximum price was set, or a range of permitted movement prescribed, and for a significant proportion state control of prices was abolished. Central wage-fixing was replaced by a system in which the bonus fund was strongly penalized for increases above the norm in the average wage paid by the enterprise (the bias thus created towards the employment of low-paid labour, in order to depress this indicator, was not unwelcome to the authorities because they feared a shake-out of such labour when the reform came into force).

In agriculture the main change introduced in 1968 was the right of collective farms to engage in non-agricultural production; by 1984 this accounted for a third of their total output (Kornai, 1986). A more subtle effect of the NEM was to consolidate the trend towards more favourable treatment of the private plot and greater freedom of decision over output. In 1969, after self-sufficiency in bread grains had been achieved, the government ceased to impose quotas for their production (which covered about 75 per cent of the area under crops). Restrictions on permitted private holdings of livestock by collective farmers were lifted, and a positive effort was made to stimulate private plot output through increased availability of credit and the encouragement of links between the private plot and the collective (the collective farm and the private plot were now officially described as an 'organic whole'). These measures have given the holders of private plots ready access to the machinery, fodder and marketing facilities of the collective. Subcontracting of livestock raising by the co-operative to its members received the green light in 1970 (Robinson, 1973).

It was recognized that in the new conditions many investments that had been made in the past would be revealed to be unprofitable. Therefore there would have to be a transition period, of perhaps ten years, before the reform could reach its final stage, during which considerable redistribution of profits through the state budget would be necessary. Despite the fact that the reform process was officially seen as a great success in the first years of operation, it began to lose momentum from about 1972, when opponents of the reform gained significant influence. As a result, the reform was frozen at a rather early point in the transition stage, and in some areas there were signs of retreat. Thus the movement towards reducing the proportion of administered prices came to a halt after 1971; the percentage of private consumption covered by free prices was 34 in 1971, and 35 in 1976, whilst the corresponding percentages for industrial producer prices were 64 and 63 respectively (Vajna, 1982). Discontent arose amongst manual workers in large state enterprises (which tended to be loss-making and therefore to pay out smaller bonuses), who felt that they were the losers from the reform process, and might even find their jobs under threat if the reform was fully completed and subsidies removed. The advocates of reform took the opposite line that its application had not been sufficiently consistent for the full benefits to be felt. However, Kádár decided that a tactical retreat was necessary. The Central Committee Plenum of November 1972 announced an increase of 8 per cent in money wages for manual workers in state industry, together with some additional controls over enterprise investment, and special ministry supervision of the fifty largest enterprises. In 1974–5 the main architects of the reform lost their leadership posts, although by that time the offensive against the reform had largely petered out and there was little agitation for further retreat (Portes, 1977).

In the macroeconomic field, the most immediate effect of the reform was to boost investment, which grew very fast in 1970 and 1971. The authorities were surprised that they were unable to restrain this by restricting bank credit, and the boom seems to have resulted from enterprises making use of profit opportunities previously hoarded in the interests of a slack plan. The funds thus created financed the investment. This boom resulted in a sharp rise in imports, so that the trade surplus with the convertible currency area that had appeared in 1969 rapidly gave way in 1970 to a large and growing deficit, which was only reduced by a sharp cutback in investment (the dollar exchange rate established at the outset of the NEM had amounted to a substantial devaluation). After 1974, however, Hungary began to run a very large balance of payments deficit against convertible currencies, and also to experience difficulties in CMEA trade. The convertible currency deficit reflected terms of trade losses, as the world market price of agricultural products fell relative to those of manufactures (Hungary was and is predominantly an exporter of agricultural products and an importer of manufactures in its convertible currency trade), and also the sharp contraction in western markets and a loss of market share, though these effects were quantitatively less important (Balassa and Tyson, 1986). The oil price increase affected Hungary substantially, but only with a lag, since the export price of Soviet oil followed CMEA pricing rules, based on a five-year moving average of world prices; this implied a continuous terms of trade loss on CMEA trade for eastern Europe throughout the 1970s. Whilst the Hungarian government did not go in for an investment boom financed by western banks in the manner of Poland, it did choose to use foreign borrowing to finance the convertible currency deficit rather than to adjust its macroeconomic stance (except for a brief period in 1976, when investment stagnated, output growth decelerated and the trade balance improved somewhat).

This policy of largely ignoring the external balance reached its apogee in 1978, when imports grew particularly fast and the trade deficit with market economies exceeded $1000 million (see table 6.1). At this point,

Table 6.1 The economic development of Hungary 1970–8

	% change over previous year								
	1970	*1971*	*1972*	*1973*	*1974*	*1975*	*1976*	*1977*	*1978*
NMP	4.9	5.9	6.2	7.0	5.9	6.1	3.0	7.1	4.0
NMP used	11.8	11.3	−3.7	2.0	12.7	6.4	1.3	6.0	9.2
Gross fixed investment	16.9	10.6	−1.1	3.2	10.9	11.5	–	12.1	4.8
Employment	0.6	0.6	0.4	0.2	0.2	0.2	−0.2	−0.2	0.2
Real wages	4.7	2.3	1.7	3.5	5.2	2.5	−0.3	3.4	3.3
Consumer prices	1.3	2.0	2.8	3.3	1.8	3.8	5.0	3.9	4.6
Trade balance with convertible currency area ($ million)	−130	−196	−72	−44	−503	−625	−420	−614	−1036

Source: UNECE (1986/7), Appendix Tables

the leadership began to accept that this stance was unsustainable, given the fast growth of the external debt and the new round of oil price increases that began at the end of 1978. In 1979 the immediate objective of macroeconomic policy was declared to be the restoration of external equilibrium. As may be seen from table 6.2, this has resulted in a prolonged period of deflation. Net material product has grown much more slowly than before, and fallen in two years (1980 and 1985), whilst NMP used (a measure of domestic absorption of resources) has decreased in most years, reflecting the transfer of resources into exports and import substitution. Employment has been falling continuously since 1979, and gross fixed investment decreased in every year from 1980 to 1985. Despite all this, the convertible currency trade deficit, which was more or less eliminated by 1984, reappeared in 1985 and 1986. There are several reasons for this, including the absence of domestic substitutes for many western imports, the high western-import content of the additional exports that have had to be sent to the USSR as a result of the second oil price increase, low world market prices for agricultural products and the deteriorating competitiveness of manufactured exports (Köves, 1986; Illés, 1986).

An assessment of the reform

A new phase of the reform began in 1979, when the party leadership announced a series of measures designed to strengthen and extend the NEM. Rather than discuss these changes at this stage, however, it is

Table 6.2 The economic development of Hungary 1979–86

	% change over previous year							
	1979	*1980*	*1981*	*1982*	*1983*	*1984*	*1985*	*1986*
NMP	1.2	−0.9	2.5	2.6	0.3	2.5	−1.4	0.5
NMP used	−5.8	−1.7	0.7	−1.1	−2.8	−0.6	−0.6	3
Gross fixed investment	0.7	−5.8	−4.3	−1.6	−3.4	−3.7	−3.0	2.3
Employment	−0.1	−1.2	−0.3	−0.6	−0.6	−0.5	−0.4	−0.6
Real wages	−3.3	−3.1	1.8	−0.4	−2.4	4.1	1.9	2.6
Real per capita incomes	−0.2	0.4	2.9	0.9	1.1	1.1	1.9	3
Consumer prices	8.9	9.1	4.6	6.9	7.3	8.3	7.0	5.3
Trade balance with convertible currency area ($ million)	−499	−564	−848	−715	−357	−74	−314	−535

Source: UNECE (1986/7), Appendix Tables

perhaps preferable to make some assessment of the original reform measures, not least because the post-1979 legislation was designed to remedy some of their perceived weaknesses.

The reform is regarded by all observers as a success in terms of matching demand and supply for consumer goods. There are goods which continue to be in short supply, such as cars, mainly because it does not seem to be official policy to abolish the queues in this case (see Kapitány et al. (1984) who show that supply responds so as to maintain a waiting list of about twice the annual delivery), but in general enterprises respond more readily to customer demands in the absence of compulsory plan indicators. The supply of food in Hungarian shops is much better and more reliable than elsewhere in eastern Europe, but the improvement extends to industrial products as well. This achievement ensures a solid basis of political support for the reform, which in turn reinforces the pro-reform elements in the party in their continuing conflict with those of a more dogmatic tendency.

At the same time there is no strong case (or at least there was no strong case in, say, 1978) for suggesting that this had been achieved at the expense of other important economic objectives, such as growth. In each of the quinquennia 1966–70 and 1971–5, NMP grew at an average rate of more than 6 per cent per annum, faster than in any other five-year period since 1950 (see table 2.4). Moreover the relaxation of price control makes it more likely that this growth was real, and not inflated by surreptitious price increases in the manner well known to administrative planning systems. The deceleration of growth after 1978 was unpleasant but not out of line with the experience of other east European countries. It is only in the mid-1980s that macroeconomic performance begins to look a little bit questionable (see table 6.2), for after the elimination of the convertible currency trade deficit in 1984, which should have provided an opportunity for some improvement, output stagnated and the trade deficit reopened in 1985–6. Moreover by this time Hungary's net foreign debt was higher than Poland's in per capita terms (but only about half as great as a percentage of convertible currency export earnings).

It has already been mentioned that little progress was made in reducing administrative control of prices during the 1970s. A major difficulty here was that the 1968 reform did little to encourage competition, so that the structure of industry remained in the highly monopolized form created for other purposes in the early 1960s. No provision was made for the splitting up of enterprises, nor was the creation of small co-operatives by groups of interested individuals made possible, whilst private sector artisans received no additional encouragement. Indeed in 1972 some successful small firms were amalgamated with larger ones, which perceived them as a threat (Marer, 1986). Thus state supervision became a necessity to prevent excessive exploitation of their market situation by large enterprises. Since foreign trade accounts for about half of Hungary's national income, import competition was potentially significant, but was restricted by tariff rates of 40–50 per cent for manufactured goods from the west, and by the non-convertibility of currencies and the system of bilateral negotiations within CMEA.

Enterprises are still owned by branch ministries. With the advent of the NEM, these ministries lost the right to instruct the enterprise over its day-to-day production decisions, but their powers are still rather greater than appears from the reform blueprint. For one thing, it is inadvisable for the enterprise to ignore the express wish of its superiors. It may suddenly find its request for credit from the central bank refused, its price-setting being scrutinized more closely, or even that it loses some subsidies or is the victim of some unpleasant new tax (I shall return to this point). Moreover, until 1985 ministries still appointed the enterprise management. In such situations, a telephone request from the ministry inevitably carries a lot of weight.

In practice, therefore, the authorities continued to have much scope for intervention in enterprise decision-making. According to Kornai (1986), only about 20 per cent of all state investment is genuinely decided at the enterprise level. Since profitability is not the only consideration, and liable to be determinant only in situations where the authorities have little interest in the decision, one would expect to see the reappearance under the NEM of many characteristics of the traditional system: soft-

Table 6.3 Variance of profitability indicators among Hungarian state enterprises in 1980 (per cent)

Sector	*Variance of original profitability*	*Variance of profitability after redistribution*
Industry	32.30	4.77
Construction	24.31	6.22
Agriculture and forestry	7.45	2.11
Transport and communication	15.09	6.46
Trade	37.49	4.89
Whole economy	29.35	5.06

Source: Kornai and Matits (1984), Table 5, p. 238

ness of budget constraints, limited relevance of financial indicators and the diversion of enterprise energy into bargaining with the authorities. Indeed one can even observe such traditional features as the hoarding of inputs and evidence of storming behaviour. Faluvégi (1986) reports that in 1981–5 industrial output in the last month of a quarter was 7–8 per cent higher than the monthly average. Enterprise stocks continue to be dominated by inputs rather than outputs, and underemployment in industry may amount to as much as 15–20 per cent of the labour force (Falus-Szikra, 1986). In short, 'the sphere of intervention of sectoral ministries in Hungary today is at least as wide as it was under the plan directive system' (Laky, 1980, p. 106).

Some research on budget constraints in Hungarian state enterprises in the late 1970s has revealed a degree of softness which surprised even the authors. Kornai and Matits (1984) found that the correlation between original profitability and profitability after redistribution (i.e. taxes and subsidies) was negligible for state enterprises in industry (0.07 in 1979 and 0.01 in 1980). In agriculture the redistributive effect was much smaller: for state farms the correlation was 0.86 in 1979 and 0.73 in 1980. However the levelling effect of taxes and subsidies was strong in all sectors (table 6.3). Clearly there is massive redistribution of profits through the state, and this is also reflected in a very high ratio of central government expenditure to GDP of over 60 per cent (Kornai, 1986). Moreover the number of days' wages paid out in bonuses is not always very closely related to post-tax profitability, and enterprises that were liquidated or absorbed by others in 1978 and 1979 did not tend to have below-average profitability. Even more striking is the fact that investment activity is, if anything, *negatively* correlated with original profitability in previous years, though it is somewhat (but not strongly) correlated with profitability after redistribution (Kornai and Matits, 1984). The natural conclusion to be drawn from this is that, far from profitability guiding the allocation of investment credits, redistribution of profits is used to help finance centrally decided investment.

On the basis of this evidence, it is difficult to believe that profit maximization could be a very meaningful objective for enterprise management, since so much was liable to be redistributed away, and the remainder might not be reflected in bonus payments in any case. What made this redistribution possible was the vast array of taxes and subsidies available to the authorities (amounting to 300 or so, according to Kornai (1986)), together with the possibility of granting *ad hoc* exemptions. With those degrees of freedom, the authorities could redistribute profits almost at will, and the impression given by the results for this period, ten to twelve years after the implementation of the reform, is that this is more or less what they were doing. The guarantees which were implicitly offered to workers in loss-making firms in the early 1970s were being allowed to remove all genuine pressures on firms to be efficient.

The effect of this is that Hungary has had difficulties similar to those of the rest of eastern Europe in achieving rapid technical progress in industry. The firm's objective function is not profitability but investment resources. Financial indicators are significant not in themselves, but as bargaining chips to be used to obtain these resources from the authorities (Hall, 1986). If one measures the technological level of Hungarian manufacturing by the value per ton of its exports, then there is clear evidence of falling behind. In 1978 value per ton was about half the world average, but there was a steady deterioration in the early 1980s, and the share of high-technology products in Hungarian exports to the west, already small, has slipped further (Illés, 1986). Other CMEA countries have had the same experience, and as we shall see in the next chapter, the growth of productivity in the post-reform Hungarian economy is very much in line with that of other CMEA countries.

A renewed reform impetus

The leadership of the Hungarian party seems to have been aware of the fact that laxity of financial discipline was undermining the objectives of the reform, for in 1977 it took a decision to introduce a new set of measures which has the appearance of at least a partial response to this. The changes began to come into effect in 1979.

A significant aspect of the new wave of reform measures is the attempt to promote a degree of competition, which is a necessary precondition for the relaxation of state supervision of enterprises. The Price Office has been instructed to formulate proposals for the elimination of monopoly positions in industry, and certain large trusts and enterprises have been broken up (Hare, 1983). In 1981 various new forms of small enterprise and co-operative organization were legalized. Small co-operatives, consisting of between 15 and 100 members, were for the first time permitted outside the agricultural sector. Self-employed persons were allowed to set up business partnerships. Groups of workers were given the opportunity to establish enterprise work teams, to which enterprises could subcontract tasks, and some independent co-operative work teams were also permitted.

Restrictions have also been lifted on the private sector. Previously a licence for private sector activity could be granted only if no similar licence had also been granted for the same neighbourhood. Now licences cannot be refused to qualified individuals, and the employment of up to seven persons is permitted. Leasing of shops and restaurants to private individuals began in 1982. The number of registered full-time workers in the private sector increased by nearly 60 per cent between 1980 and 1984, and this sector more than doubled its share of national income between 1978 and 1983. There is also a great deal of moonlighting and part-time private work, not to mention unrecorded activities (which were estimated at about 8 per cent of national income according to one team of researchers – *The Guardian*, 10 August 1987). The striking thing about this 'second economy' activity is how many people are involved in it. When household plots of collective farmers and other petty market gardening production are included, as many as three-quarters of Hungarian families may perform some second economy work (Révész, 1986).

It can be seen from table 6.2 that from 1979 to 1984 real wages fell quite sharply, whilst real per capita incomes continued to increase. Thus the expansion of the private sector was important in mitigating the effects of the fall in the real wage in the state sector in this period (the per capita income figures also reflect a relatively strong performance from agriculture, which grew faster than the rest of the economy at this time).

Rates of pay in the private sector tend to be high, even for employees: two to three times that in state enterprises, and the same ratio applies to contract work done by enterprise work teams (Falus-Szikra, 1986). The fast expansion of the private sector suggests that an equilibrium has not yet been reached, so the sector benefits from excess demand for its services. However it is not certain how much the ratio of private sector to public sector incomes would fall in any case. State sector wages are depressed by surplus staff and poor labour discipline (there is a very high rate of labour turnover), and state sector employment affords contacts and access to machinery and materials that is vital to much moonlighting activity, so that the remuneration of this activity includes an important element of payment for the favourable status of the worker rather than for the work itself (Kenedi (1981) offers an interesting insight into this in the construction sector, where it is particularly rife). Since private sector entrepreneurs have little opportunity to reinvest their profits and fear a possible clampdown on their activities, they tend to indulge in luxury consumption, which causes some political reaction against them.

In the mid-1980s these attempts to stimulate competition were supplemented by a series of others designed to harden budget constraints. Branch ministries lost the right to appoint enterprise managers, who were henceforth to be selected by the employees of the enterprise. Taxation of profits has been reduced, and a value-added tax and an income tax came into force at the beginning of 1988. More generally, the intention is to reduce subsidies on consumer goods, and to raise retail prices relative to wholesale prices. The number of enterprises with the right to engage directly in foreign trade has been increased. A market in government bonds has been initiated, and there is serious consideration of a form of stock market which would enable enterprises to invest in each other, rather than having to invest in themselves simply for lack of any other outlet. It is possible that the commercial banking functions of the central bank will be spread amongst a number of separate and competing banking institutions. This would represent a major move away from the traditional 'mono-bank' structure, in an attempt to enhance the role of strictly commercial criteria in credit allocation.

In sum, there are some moves towards tightening financial discipline, but few economists in Hungary would argue that they represent more than a partial shift way from a basically administrative system of economic regulation. According to Laszlo Antal in a 1985 interview, subsidies are being eliminated by increasing prices to customers with the tacit support of the authorities, rather than by cost-cutting; 82 per cent of profits are still taxed away, and enterprise behaviour continues to be dominated by bargaining with the authorities for various kinds of subsidy (Hall, 1986). The phenomenon of investment hunger therefore persists as strongly as ever.

Conclusions

The main achievement of the Hungarian reform lies in abolishing directive planning and substituting a direct relationship between supplier and customer. This has resulted in greater responsiveness of supply to customer needs, and permanently increased the decision-making powers of enterprises, so that these are now significantly greater than in other

CMEA countries. However, in industry budget constraints remain very soft. This is reflected in a lack of concern about the profitability of investment, a continued tendency towards over-investment and hence shortages of materials, and a sluggish rate of technical progress. The monopolistic structure of Hungarian industry necessitates state supervision to prevent exploitation of market power by enterprises. The small size of the economy makes this difficult to abandon, unless other CMEA members undertake similar reforms, not only because in many cases effective competition can only come from imports, but also because enterprises producing for export to CMEA countries are tightly constrained by the system of foreign trade negotiations.

In agriculture the reform has been significantly more successful. The supply of food to the shops is much improved, and Hungary is the only member of the Soviet bloc that is a net exporter of grain. Between 1965 and 1982, agricultural production per head increased faster than in any other east European country (Lazarcik, 1986). This reflects the much harder budget constraints in this field, and a much more positive attitude towards the private sector. Although Hungarian agriculture is similar in its institutional structure to that of the USSR, with large collective farms incorporating small household plots and private livestock holdings, the co-operative has significantly greater freedom of decision over output in Hungary, and government policy has aimed to develop a fruitful relationship between private and co-operative production. In the USSR, collective farms (and private plots to an even greater extent) have long suffered from the stigma of representing less than a fully socialist form of organization; in Hungary this impediment to their development was abandoned in the 1960s.

As table 6.2 shows, Hungary has experienced significant inflation in the 1980s. If this is a price to be paid for reform, it might turn out to be a high one. Inflation of more than about 5 per cent per annum is liable to generate considerable anxiety. In fact the price record of the Hungarian reform was good up to 1975. Since then, price stability has been sacrificed to the objectives of reducing consumer price subsidies and depressing real wages. The leadership has judged it more politic to push up the rate of inflation than to depress the rate of increase of money wages. It is probably true that the reform has eased the way for such a policy, since the government is no longer the sole price setter, but there seems to be no reason to conclude that economic reform *necessarily* results in inflation.

Since the Hungarian reform seems to have several positive features and few demonstrably negative ones, why has it not been more widely imitated? We shall come back to this point in chapter 9. Suffice it to say for the moment that in Hungary the events of 1956 created an unusually favourable environment for economic reform. With the road to political change so obviously blocked, there was a tacit acceptance that experimentation in the economic field offered a possible substitute. Kádár benefited from a feeling that the alternatives could only be worse. In this situation a carefully conceived package of reform measures could only strengthen his political position; there was little danger of arousing popular expectations of more fundamental change that could not be met. In the later 1980s, there are some signs of a breakdown in this social consensus around the reform process. The restraints imposed by 1956 are fading after three decades, and frustration at the slow speed of change is mounting. The Hungarian reform faces an important and difficult period ahead.

7

East-West Comparisons

Introduction

In this chapter I undertake some comparisons of the economic performance of eastern Europe and the Soviet Union with that of other countries. My concern is with *economic* measures of welfare. I do not consider factors such as freedom of information or racial discrimination, which may be of great importance to the quality of life of many individuals, but are primarily non-economic. The comparison covers consumer satisfaction, equality of income distribution, unemployment, inflation and growth. A section is devoted to each.

Consumer satisfaction

On consumer satisfaction there is little doubt that the socialist economies come off worse. In capitalist economies direct competition between producers encourages them to respond to consumer desires. Even in oligopolistic markets, where price competition may not be strong, this is frequently offset by substantial non-price competition. Quality and design characteristics are of major importance for more durable items, and it is a matter of serious concern for a company if its products obtain a reputation for inferior design or materials. Although everybody can cite cases where prices seem unjustifiably high, there are equally many cases of markets where competition is obviously intense.

In centrally planned economies the satisfaction of consumer demand in terms of quantities is undertaken by the planners; more detailed specification of product lines is left to negotiation between the retailers and the suppliers. We have already seen the disadvantages of this arrangement from the customer's point of view in earlier chapters. It is practically impossible for retail organizations to predict the demand for each size and variety of shoe from each outlet in advance and to write the correct amounts into contracts with suppliers. Thus even exact fulfilment of the contract will not prevent particular shortages from occurring. Some degree of flexibility of supply in response to fluctuations of demand is highly desirable. But any such flexibility gives suppliers scope for fulfilling their plan without paying attention to demand. Contracts which specify only a total number of children's shoes invite producers to sacrifice variety to economy by producing long runs of one type. This problem is greatly exacerbated by the tendency towards excess demand in consumer goods markets. As Kornai (1959) stresses, the relative bargaining position of suppliers and customers varies greatly with the degree of shortage of the product. If supplies are plentiful, purchasers can send back deliveries which do not correspond to their requirements with a reasonable expectation of obtaining what they want. If supplies are short, purchasers may be forced to accept what they are offered. They still have the option of returning the goods, but if they do they may simply be pushed to the back of the buying queue and get nothing; if they keep the goods, they at least have the possibility of bartering with others in the hope of obtaining something closer to what they originally ordered.

The recent Soviet idea of making enterprise bonuses dependent on contract fulfilment is designed to give customers more hold over suppliers. Unless 98 per cent of the contracts are fulfilled, the bonus is lost. However the whole system depends on customers being willing to report underfulfilment. If the market situation favours the suppliers, this may not be the case. The customers then know that, if they report underfulfilment, the suppliers have strong possibilities of retaliating in future periods by delaying supplies, ignoring requests and so forth. Moreover the plan has committed the customer to the supplier. In such a situation, the customers are likely to conclude that, unless the supplier's performance has been far below the norm, they have more to lose by complaining about the supplier to the authorities than by keeping quiet. The performance of an alternative supplier may be little better, and the customer will rapidly gain a poor reputation amongst suppliers. Thus it is likely that customers will tacitly accept a degree of contract underfulfilment which they perceive as normal in current market conditions, and the sanction of making bonuses dependent on contract fulfilment will not have a marked effect.

Centrally planned economies also have difficulties over the quality of goods. The quotation given in chapter 3 about how television sets are put together in periods of storming is indicative of this. In 1986 Gorbachev made a speech in which he said that many of the goods available in the shops were of such poor quality that they could only continue to be produced in a socialist economy: in a capitalist economy the manufacturers would have gone bust long ago. The problem is that producing enterprises have an incentive to make life easy for themselves by producing goods of the lowest quality acceptable; because quality is hard to measure, the acceptable level may be rather low. Some aspects, such as the quality of materials used, can be measured, and the incentive system may actually encourage quality in this respect, since the use of more expensive materials boosts the product price and hence sales revenue. The introduction of price surcharges for higher-quality goods has probably encouraged this tendency further. But aspects of quality such as durability, reliability or adaptation of design to customer requirements are less easily measurable and therefore tend to go unrewarded. It is difficult to see what method of quality certification could provide an enterprise with a significant incentive to increase the average length of life of washing machine motors, for example. Verification would be a costly process requiring sampling of machines in use many years after manufacture, and so the results could scarcely be entered into enterprise bonus functions at the time the improvements were made. The short time horizons imposed on enterprises by the planning system is the major source of difficulty here.

The planners might attempt to correct for this by observing more closely what happens in the market place, for example whether customers always choose washing machine A in preference to B, and whether B only sells when A is out of stock. The difficulty comes in translating this information into the appropriate planning signals to enterprises. How should the producers of A be rewarded and those of B penalized? Social commitments make it difficult to imitate the market mechanism and replace all production of B by A, for if the factory producing B is not to make washing machines nor to sack workers, what is it to make instead? Is there any guarantee that it would do any better at the alternatives? At least it already has the equipment to produce washing machines. In practice these social considerations mean that the producers of B will probably get away with a reprimand and an exhortation to learn from A. This underlines the point that it is not possible to make implicit social commitments to the population as producers which do not have ramifications for their experience as consumers.

In general shopping is a more frustrating experience in eastern Europe than it is in the west. Queuing is all-pervasive in the Soviet Union, but less frequent elsewhere. Nevertheless the disappearance of certain goods from the shops for long periods of time seems to be a widespread phenomenon. From this author's observations in the summer of 1973, for example, fresh vegetables were more or less unobtainable in Czechoslovakia and fresh fruit was unobtainable in the GDR. One might expect queue and search times to reflect difficulties in finding goods, although of course if they are known to be absent altogether no time will be spent in hunting for them. Pryor (1977) presents evidence on average shopping times in various countries using data collected in 1965–6. These data seem to indicate longer shopping times in eastern Europe, particularly in Poland and the USSR. However, in Pryor's statistical analysis, this could more or less be explained by the relatively small proportion of the population employed in the wholesale and retail trade in the Soviet bloc.

If this were true, it would imply that if east European countries devoted a higher proportion of the labour force to distribution, shopping times would be similar to those in capitalist countries at similar income levels. However this seems to conflict with some other evidence. According to Turcan's (1977) observations in Wrocław in Poland, there was no shortage of staff in shops, but the employees showed no great interest in selling. Queues were frequent and the service was poor. Turcan frequently observed staff standing around, apparently doing nothing, whilst customers were waiting to be served. He attributes this to the fact that staff are collectively responsible for losses from theft, and indeed had the right to call for a stock-taking should any one of their number leave. Presumably the staff who were apparently doing nothing were guarding against theft by customers (Turcan cites the example of a football, which a customer had picked up and examined, being moved out of reach by sales staff).

In short, in virtually every aspect of consumption (quality of product, availability, and shopping time) the consumer in the Soviet bloc has a more difficult time than his or her counterpart in the west.

Unemployment

In the 1960s the advanced capitalist countries were more or less in a state of full employment. Measured unemployment rates were very low, and could be accounted for by frictional or structural factors. However, the inflationary crisis of the early 1970s has pushed these countries into more cautious demand management policies, as a result of which economic growth has moderated and unemployment has increased rather sharply. Few economists would attempt to deny that unemployment in western Europe today contains a substantial involuntary component which reflects depressed demand conditions.

The socialist countries of eastern Europe, by contrast, claimed long ago that they had eliminated unemployment. Unemployment benefits are unavailable, and a man who cannot show proof of full-time employment comes under immediate suspicion for black market or criminal activities (this is less true for a woman, as it is accepted that many women are not in paid employment because of family responsibilities). If an enterprise is forced to dismiss a part of its workforce, it is obliged to help those workers to find alternative employment. How true is this claim to have eliminated unemployment?

There is little doubt that it is substantially true. As a result of taut plans and the desire of enterprises to hoard inputs, the normal state of the labour market is excess demand. Indeed socialist managers frequently complain about the lack of discipline, absenteeism and instability of the labour force that result from this. The strength of the demand for labour is reflected in activity rates that are 10–15 per cent higher than in west European countries at a similar stage of development, mainly because of the much higher degree of participation of women in paid employment (Kornai, 1982, table B7). At the same time there is considerable underemployment on the job, in the sense that production is not infrequently interrupted because of a shortage of materials, and the enterprise may have successfully built into its plans a cushion of excess labour. In the Hungarian press there have appeared estimates that up to one-third of the labour force is surplus to requirements. Thus there is still underutilization of labour in the system; it just does not take the form of overt unemployment. However labour slack of this kind does not have the social and economic stigma that attaches to involuntary unemployment. The people involved have full-time work and the status and earnings that go with it. The slack merely means that they also benefit from an easy time at work as well. Ultimately, of course, they pay for it in lower living standards than they might otherwise have had, but these losses are distributed more evenly than are the output losses associated with unemployment under capitalism, whose effects fall very largely on the unemployed.

Income distribution

Most developed countries publish data of some kind on income distribution, but making international comparisons is another question. Differences in the scope of the sample and the processing of the data often make direct comparison difficult (for a summary of the problems, see Wiles, 1978). Economists have typically been interested in two sorts of distribution: one which measures the standard of living of individuals or households (derived from tax data or sample surveys), and one which measures the dispersion of labour incomes (typically obtained from a sample of data provided by employers). These latter data often exclude significant sections of the working population (e.g. the self-employed, those who work in agriculture, the military), but are generally more reliable for what they do cover. Sample surveys of households attempt to obtain a picture of standards of living for the entire population, but in eastern Europe the results are presented per capita (that is, household income is divided by the number of persons) whereas in the west it is more usual to treat the household as a unit. This distribution will be affected not only by the incomes of those excluded from the samples of wage- and salary-earners but also by variations in the number of earners per household (in the west) or in the proportion of earners per household (in the east).

It would appear that the advent of socialism tends to be associated with an equalization in the distribution of income, not just between classes but also within the class of wage- and salary-earners. Thus in the USSR the distribution of income amongst manual workers in manufacturing industry was significantly more equal in 1928 than in 1914, and in Hungary, Czechoslovakia and Poland from 1945 to 1948 wage dispersion was greatly reduced, higher incomes leveled down and peasant incomes raised (Lydall, 1968; Kende and Strmiska, 1984). It is Stalin who stands out as the one effective opponent of these equalizing tendencies. The new pay scales introduced in the USSR in 1931 considerably increased wage dispersion, especially at the upper end of the scale where the previous equalizing tendencies had had the most marked effect, so that by the time of Stalin's death income distribution was markedly less equal in the USSR than in eastern Europe (Stalin's determination to keep peasant incomes low also contributed to this). But Stalin's successors reversed this policy, raising collective farm incomes and reducing wage dispersion, so that by the mid-1960s there was little difference in income inequality between the USSR and eastern Europe (Wiles and Markowski, 1971).

One of the features of wage distribution in eastern Europe is that non-manual workers have little advantage over manual workers. In Czechoslovakia in 1965, a lawyer earned less than a train-driver. Figures from 1973 show that average non-manual earnings exceeded manual earnings by 18 per cent in Hungary, 20 per cent in Czechoslovakia and 29 per cent in Poland. Despite a commitment to equal pay, average female wages in these three countries have remained around two-thirds of average male wages since 1949, despite a continuous reduction in the qualifications differential. The worst-paid employees are generally found in the tertiary sector, and there is a correlation between the proportion of women in a sector and low wages (Kende and Strmiska, 1984).

One of the traditional claims of the socialist movement is that socialism would overcome the regional inequalities that are characteristic of capitalism. In fact most of the countries of eastern Europe are too small for regional differences to be very marked. The one exception is Yugoslavia, whose performance in this regard is discussed in the next chapter. In 1917 the Russian empire comprised some well developed areas and some very backward ones, such as Central Asia, which was still inhabited to a large extent by nomads. Under Soviet rule quite a lot of regional equalization has been achieved. The ordering is much the same, with the Baltic republics at the top and Central Asia at the bottom, but the spread has been reduced to a factor of about two. There is little doubt that a comparison of the economic development of the Transcaucasian or Central Asian republics of the USSR with that of neighbouring areas of Turkey or Iran would be highly favourable to the Soviet Union.

In capitalist countries there is a tendency for the distribution of income to become more equal as the country develops. Thus the degree of inequality tends to be less in the UK or Canada than in Spain or Turkey, for example. There is little sign of a similar tendency in eastern Europe. Romania, one of the least developed countries, has one of the smallest wage dispersions, and in the mid-1970s the greatest wage inequality was in Poland (Askanas and Levcik, 1983). Nor is there any consistent trend in wage dispersion over time. Dispersion appears to have been reduced between the mid-1960s and mid-1970s in the USSR, the GDR and Bulgaria, increased in Romania, Hungary and Poland, and remained approximately unchanged in Czechoslovakia (Askanas and Levcik, 1983; Michal, 1978).

Amongst east European economists it is a quite widely held view that the dispersion of wages is too narrow from an incentive viewpoint, and the widening of the dispersion in Hungary and Poland reflected some deliberate policy moves in this direction. It is a little surprising, therefore, to find that wage dispersion in eastern Europe is not so dissimilar to that of advanced western countries, as far as can be judged.[1] Askanas and Levcik (1983) report that wage dispersion in Austria is intermediate between Czechoslovakia and Poland (provided it is assumed that the lowest Austrian observations can be discarded as representing part-timers), and Wiles and Markowski (1971, fig. 7) demonstrate that 1966 UK wage and salary dispersion was not markedly greater than in Poland and the USSR. A similar result for the USSR is reported by Bergson (1984). It is when the sample is extended to include non-employees that the performance of socialist countries begins to look significantly better. This is because capitalist economies contain some households with very large property incomes. Thus according to the estimates of Wiles (1978, Table 7.17) for post-tax per capita income, the five socialist countries all have a more equal income distribution than the six capitalist countries included in the sample, and there is remarkably little difference between them. Various sources of distortion need to be assessed, however, such as: the exclusion of the private sector and high party officials from the socialist countries' statistics, the impact of benefits in kind and differences in pricing systems.

There is scant information on private sector incomes in socialist countries, but in most cases the sector is too small to cause any alteration to our general judgement about the equality of income distribution. One country with a sizeable private sector is Poland, because its agriculture is not collectivized. A 1967 sample survey of Polish farmers, quoted by Wiles and Markowski (1971, Table 15), revealed a lower mean income than in the socialized sector of the economy, but with a similar spread. Kende and Strmiska (1984) argue that the small size of holdings has prevented the peasantry in Poland from improving its relative position in the income distribution as in Czechoslovakia and Hungary. As a result of recent expansion the private sector in Hungary has now reached a size where it might have a significant effect on income distribution. A large proportion of the population has some involvement with it, but opportunities are certainly unequally distributed. For example, it is known that in the medical sector low official incomes are substantially supplemented by a well-established system of bribes. It seems likely that the expansion of the private sector has increased the dispersion of income, but this effect would have to be implausibly large for the dispersion to be as great as in market economies at a similar level of development.

High officials in socialist countries typically receive a considerable quantity of benefits in kind to supplement salaries which are not exceptional. The émigré Michael Voslensky (1984) has painted a colourful picture of the life of the party official in the late Brezhnev era, as part of an argument that the bureaucracy now forms a new ruling class. He describes in lurid detail the wonders of the Kremlin canteen, the special shopping facilities and the dachas which insulate the rulers from ordinary life, and the periodic envelopes full of bank notes which are issued to supplement salaries. Nevertheless, because of the absence of property ownership a highly-remunerated socialist official still receives far less income than the wealthiest households in the west, and because the number of officials who receive these privileges is not very great, it is generally believed that such privileges make little difference to overall income distribution.

The tendency in eastern Europe to subsidize basic foods and compensate for this by having high turnover tax rates on luxury goods is likely to have some equalizing effect on the distribution of income. On the other hand all studies of subsidized housing carried out since 1960 indicate that

Table 7.1 Consumer price inflation 1970–86

	% change over previous year						
Year	*Bulgaria*	*Czechoslovakia*	*GDR*	*Hungary*	*Poland*	*Romania*	*USSR*
Average 1970–5	0.1	0.3	−0.3	2.5	2.2	0.5	0
1976	0.3	0.9	0.0	5.0	4.7	0.7	0
1977	0.4	1.4	−0.1	3.9	4.9	0.5	0
1978	1.5	1.5	−0.1	4.6	8.7	1.6	1
1979	4.5	3.0	0.3	8.9	6.7	2.0	1
1980	14.0	3.4	0.4	9.1	9.1	2.1	1
1981	0.4	0.9	0.2	4.6	24.4	2.0	1
1982	0.3	4.7	0.0	6.9	101.5	16.9	3
1983	1.4	1.1	0.0	7.3	23.0	5.2	1
1984	0.7	0.9	0.0	8.3	15.7	1.1	−1
1985	1.7	1.3	0.0	7.0	14.4	0.4	1
1986		0.4		5.3	18.0		

Source: UNECE (1986/7), Appendix Table B6

it is inegalitarian in its effects (Kende and Strmiska, 1984; for Hungary, see Daniel, 1985). This is because of the tendency to use offers of housing as an attraction to scarce labour in an economy where too large a differential in money incomes is politically unacceptable. This results in the higher-paid strata obtaining the greatest housing subsidies, since they are allocated the best state housing, whilst the lower-paid occupational groups are more likely to be owner-occupiers (Szelenyi, 1983). This inegalitarian pattern asserts itself even in an urban environment; it is reinforced by the fact that agricultural workers, who tend to be concentrated at the lower end of the income distribution, mostly own their own houses. Kende and Strmiska also quote the results of a 1979 Hungarian study which found that benefits in kind in general tend to be less equally distributed than money incomes.

Nevertheless, even when full allowance is made for all these possible inaccuracies, it seems clear that the socialist countries have achieved a distribution of income which is more equal than that of capitalist countries at a similar stage of development, and at least as equal as that of the most advanced capitalist countries.

Inflation

The official record of consumer price inflation in European socialist countries is shown in table 7.1. Up to about 1975 these figures certainly lend support to the claim that these countries suffer less from inflation than their western counterparts. Since then there has been a certain deterioration. The GDR and the Soviet Union continue to claim more or less stable prices. In Bulgaria and Romania inflation has been very mild except for one brief period (1979–80 and 1982–3 respectively). In Czechoslovakia the inflation rate has been slightly greater, although still no more than a creep. But Hungary now seems locked into inflation rates of between 4 and 10 per cent per annum, and Poland has experienced double-digit inflation since 1981, with prices doubling in one year in 1982.

How accurate are these figures? The consensus amongst those who have studied this matter is that they tend to underestimate the degree of inflation i.e. there is a certain amount of 'hidden inflation' which does not appear in the official statistics. The question of hidden inflation has wider ramifications, because constant price series for components of national income are derived by dividing a current price series by a price index series. If the price index series underestimates inflation by x per cent, this will mean that real output growth is overestimated by x per cent. As we shall see in the next section, this is a matter of some importance when comparing growth rates in east and west.

How does hidden inflation arise? It occurs not because the statisticians fiddle the numbers (the tendency in these countries is to suppress uncomfortable statistics rather than to falsify them, at least at governmental level), but because of the way in which the indices are calculated. In centrally planned economies, the bulk of prices are fixed centrally. The statisticians use these officially prescribed prices to calculate the price indices. If no price in the price manuals is altered, the officially recorded rate of inflation is zero. However, things may be a little different on the ground. For the enterprise, an increase in profitability is desirable, other things being equal, because it tends to improve bonuses. Therefore the enterprise has an incentive to reduce costs on a product whose price has already been set, and to put in bogus claims about improvements to back an appeal for a rise in prices. Both these phenomena are well known in centrally planned economies. Sometimes a supposedly improved product is introduced at a higher price, and the previous version mysteriously becomes unavailable. Alternatively, the materials used are gradually downgraded in quality over time, so after a number of years it is necessary to pay more for items of the same quality. The scope for this game obviously expands with the complexity of the product. It is hard to play it with food, but relatively easy with consumer durables and machinery. The statisticians ignore this phenomenon in their calculations because, according to the rules, the price-setting agencies should be preventing it from happening.

Table 7.2 Hidden inflation in the GDR as estimated by Keren

Period	*Hidden inflation (% p.a.)*
1950–5	4.0
1955–60	2.2
1960–5	0
1965–70	0
1970–3	0.4
1973–7	2.9
1977–81	2.6

Source: Keren (1987)

For all industrial products in the USSR, Steiner (1982) estimates hidden inflation at about 1 per cent per annum. Howard (1976) obtains a similar estimate for consumer prices from 1955 to 1972. Hanson (1984) quotes a slightly higher figure estimate by Schroeder and Denton, of 1.6 per cent per annum over the period 1960 to 1975. For eastern Europe, comparisons of prices of similar baskets of consumption goods in socialist and capitalist economies at different points in time seem to indicate a rate of hidden inflation that is slightly higher than this. Keren (1977) quotes a figure of 1.5 per cent per annum for the GDR, based on a comparison with West Germany. In a later study (1987), he estimates rates of hidden inflation in the GDR as given in table 7.2. An official study carried out by the Austrian and Polish statistical offices between 1964 and 1978 implies a rate of hidden consumer price inflation in Poland of 2.3 per cent per annum, although this rate was not uniform over the period. For 1964 to 1973 hidden inflation was only 0.8 per cent per annum, accelerating to 5 per cent per annum from 1973 to 1978 (Askanas and Laski, 1985). This latter figure may be untypical, reflecting the special conditions of Poland in that period. Havlik (1985) reports the results of a price comparison for a basket of consumption goods bought in Austria and Czechoslovakia in 1980, and compares them with the results of a similar study carried out by the Economic Institute of the Czech Academy of Sciences in 1964. Assuming the Austrian price index to be correct, the Czech rate of consumer price inflation emerges as 3.3 per cent per annum, compared with an official figure of 1.4 per cent per annum.

Overall, then, hidden inflation in the consumer goods sector probably amounts to 1–2 per cent per annum in centrally planned economies. Because enterprises in Hungary have been given significantly greater freedom to set their own prices since the reform, it is likely that hidden inflation is less significant there. However the problem of open inflation now seems to be at least as great in Hungary as in the west, and the same is true of Poland, which since 1982 has moved some way towards the Hungarian model. It seems that economic reform, by reducing the government's immediate responsibility for price setting, removes some of the political restraints against allowing excess demand to reveal itself in price increases.

Growth

To which other areas should the growth rates of eastern Europe be compared? There is considerable evidence that growth rates vary with the level of development, and in particular that countries which are within a certain distance of the most advanced states have the opportunity of faster growth by technological catching up (Gomulka, 1986). Thus it would not be correct, for example, to compare the USSR with the USA, as Soviet propagandists have been prone to do over the years, because the USA is too far ahead in development. More defensible is a comparison with western Europe, but in 1950 the income levels of eastern Europe and the USSR were more on a par with the less developed countries of southern Europe such as Spain. The United Nations Economic Commission for Europe classifies Portugal, Spain, Yugoslavia, Greece and Turkey as belonging to southern Europe. Since this is a rather small and differentiated group, it seems useful to make some comparisons with industrialized western Europe as well.

Table 7.3 presents some figures on growth rates in different parts of Europe from 1950 to 1969. For eastern Europe and the USSR, the UNECE estimates are straightforward conversions of official NMP figures to GDP by adding in estimates of depreciation and the output of the non-material sphere (NMP growth rates are 0–1 per cent higher than GDP growth rates). This calculation results in a growth rate for eastern Europe and the USSR similar to that of southern Europe, and somewhat higher than for industrialized western Europe (however it is noticeable that the trend is different: in the east growth decelerated in the 1960s, whereas the rest of Europe experienced an acceleration). The Alton computations are based on physical output indicators rather than official NMP figures. For Yugoslavia his results agree with those of the UN, but for the rest of eastern Europe his estimates are noticeably lower. The difference is probably accounted for by hidden price increases, which would inflate official NMP growth figures but not physical indicators (which measure total numbers of radio sets produced rather than their value divided by an official price index). This procedure may

Table 7.3 Growth rates of GDP per person employed 1950–69 (per cent per annum)

	UNECE estimates			*Alton estimates*
	1950/2–67/9	*1950/2–58/60*	*1958/60–67/9*	*1950–67*
Bulgaria	6.4	5.7	7.0	
Czechoslovakia	4.0	4.7	3.5	2.5
GDR	5.3	6.4	4.4	4.0
Hungary	3.8	2.9	4.8	3.2
Poland	4.2	4.4	4.0	2.6
Romania	6.2	4.8	7.6	5.0
USSR	5.5	6.3	4.7	
Eastern Europe + USSR	5.2	5.8	4.7	
Industrialized				
Western Europe	3.9	3.6	4.2	
Southern Europe	5.2	4.6	5.8	
of which Yugoslavia	5.4	5.9	5.0	5.4

Sources: UNECE (1971), Part I, p. 6
T.P. Alton, 'Economic structure and growth in eastern Europe', in US Congress Joint Economic Committee, *Economic Developments in Countries of Eastern Europe*, Washington: US Government Printing Office, 1970

underestimate growth rates in so far as it fails to take account of quality improvements.

Table 7.4 shows the growth rate of real output per person employed in various parts of Europe since 1966. Eastern European figures are based on official statistics for NMP; since the difference in growth rates between the material and non-material sectors was lower in this period, adjustment to GDP would produce only marginal alterations. In western Europe growth was virtually nil during the sharp recession of 1974–5; alternative calculations breaking the series at 1973 rather than 1975 show the effect of placing the cut-off point before rather than after this recession. The most striking feature of the table is that all parts of Europe experienced a very marked deceleration of growth in the second decade. As far as comparisons between different regions is concerned, the results shown in table 7.4 tend to support those in table 7.3: in both periods, according to official figures, growth tended to be slightly higher in eastern Europe than in the more advanced areas of western Europe, and very similar to that of southern European countries (of which Yugoslavia constitutes something of an exception, to be discussed in the next chapter). Once again, however, this conclusion has to be tempered by recognition that growth rates for eastern Europe are likely to be exaggerated.

Table 7.4 Growth rates of output per person employed 1966–85 (per cent per annum)

Eastern Europe (net material product per person employed)

	1966–75	*1976–85*
Bulgaria	7.8	4.6
Czechoslovakia	5.0	1.9
GDR	5.1	3.7
Hungary	5.6	2.5
Poland	5.9	0.0
Romania	9.2	5.5
Eastern Europe	6.1	2.6 (3.5 excl. Poland)
USSR	6.4	2.8

Western Europe (gross domestic product per person employed)

	1966–75	*1976–85*	*1966–73*	*1974–85*
France, FRG, Italy, UK	3.5	2.1	4.3	1.8
OECD Europe	3.5	2.0	4.2	1.8
Greece	5.7	1.5	7.7	1.4
Portugal	5.1	2.9	6.9	2.3
Spain	5.2	3.3	7.0	3.4
Yugoslavia	3.3	−0.1	3.9	0.1

Sources: UNECE (1976), Part II p. 19
UNECE (1986/7), Appendix Tables
OECD Economic Outlook 41 (June 1987), Table R3
OECD, *Economic Survey of Yugoslavia* (various years)

Western recomputations of east European growth over the period 1966–84 are shown in table 7.5. They suggest a growth rate only about half as great as the official figures – a reduction of about 3 per cent per annum for 1966–75 and about 2 per cent per annum for 1976–84 (when Poland is excluded). As in the period up to 1967, these recomputations suggest that east European growth rates were slightly below those of western Europe, not consistently above them as table 7.4 implies. But these western calculations may have some downward bias as a result of neglecting quality improvements. One independent check on this is to see whether the difference between official and western growth rate calculations is consistent with estimates of hidden inflation derived from other sources.

Table 7.5 Alternative estimates of east European productivity growth 1966–84

	Growth rates of GNP per person employed (% p.a.) 1966–75	1976–84
Bulgaria	3.7	1.1
Czechoslovakia	2.0	1.1
GDR	3.0	1.2
Hungary	2.2	2.2
Poland	2.6	0.7
Romania	4.9	2.7
Eastern Europe*	3.0	1.3 (1.6 excl. Poland)

* 1980 GNP weights
Source: T.P. Alton, 'East European GNPs: Origins of Product, Final Uses, Rates of Growth, and International Comparisons', in US Congress Joint Economic Committee (1986), Vol. 1

It was mentioned in the previous section that hidden inflation in the consumer goods sector probably amounts on average to 1–2 per cent per annum – perhaps more in the less developed economies of Romania and Bulgaria, and probably less in Hungary since the reform, where the scope for open price increases is greater. It is widely believed that the problem is significantly greater for investment goods, because a new piece of equipment is seldom an exact replica of an old one (this view has recently been challenged by Bergson (1987) but see the replies by Nove and Hanson in the same issue of *Soviet Studies*).[2] To put a figure on hidden inflation in the investment goods sector is very difficult. Steiner (1982) studied the Soviet machine-building industry, and claims that between 1960 and 1975 prices rose by more than 40 per cent, whereas the official index shows a fall of almost 25 per cent. This implies a discrepancy of over 4 per cent per annum, and Steiner provides quotes from Soviet authors which suggest substantial agreement with his conclusions. Nove (1981) cites further articles in the Soviet economic press which indicate that the problem is at least as great as Steiner suggests, and which also claim that there is similar hidden inflation in construction costs. Further argument along these lines has been provided by Wiles (1982) and Hanson (1984), but reliable quantification remains elusive. If 3 per cent per annum is a reasonable guesstimate for investment goods, then we have something like 2 per cent per annum hidden inflation for NMP as a whole to be subtracted from official growth rates. From tables 7.3 to 7.5, we can see that western recomputations tend to reduce official growth rate figures by 1–3 per cent per annum. Thus these recomputations are not inconsistent with the information that we have about hidden inflation. Overall, this seems to suggest that eastern Europe is just about maintaining its productivity level relative to that of western Europe, or may be lagging behind slightly. It is not catching up with the west, as southern European countries gradually are. This is consistent with the evidence presented in chapter 4 that there are significant impediments to technical progress at enterprise level in centrally planned economies.

The Five-Year Plans for 1986–90 indicate that pre-1975 growth rates are now regarded as unattainable in eastern Europe. The Soviet Union plans NMP growth of 4.3 per cent per annum, compared with an outturn for 1981–5 of 3.6 per cent, and eastern Europe plans an average of 5.2 per cent per annum (UNECE, 1986/7, Table 4.1.5). This seems to represent a widespread recognition that the growth slowdown has systemic causes and is permanent. Indeed it is probable that the possibilities for an acceleration of growth are now greater in western than in eastern Europe. The unemployment rate in the EEC averaged 11.4 per cent in 1985 compared with 4.3 per cent in 1975, and the investment ratio has fallen from an average of 22.7 per cent in OECD Europe in 1966–75 to under 20 per cent in each year since 1982, whereas investment ratios have scarcely fallen at all in eastern Europe, as table 2.6 shows (*OECD Economic Outlook* 40, Table R3; 41, Table R12). Although careful adjustment for differences in pricing practice does not indicate that investment ratios are systematically higher in eastern than in western Europe, there would seem to be only very limited scope in current conditions for raising them further, and plans for the period up to 1990 reflect this.

Conclusions

The broad conclusion that emerges from this analysis is that the socialist economies of eastern Europe and the USSR have a better record than their western counterparts on unemployment, equality of income distribution and inflation (at least where prices are centrally administered), but a distinctly poorer one on consumer satisfaction and a marginally poorer one on economic growth. Although socialist economies have grown at reasonable rates by pre-war standards, they have not quite been able to match the acceleration of growth achieved by the rest of Europe since 1945. Eastern European growth rates reached their nadir in 1981–2; they have since recovered somewhat, but the evidence suggests that further improvements in growth and consumer satisfaction are dependent on the implementation of far-reaching reforms. Quite apart from the issue of their political acceptability, such reforms seem likely to imply some loss of the price stability, income equality and even security of employment currently enjoyed.

Notes

1 This discrepancy might be explained by the fact that wage dispersion in eastern Europe, though quantitatively as great as in the west, is less well related to economic performance.
2 This is also the reason why I use labour productivity alone as a measure of technical progress. If hidden inflation is greater for investment goods than for output as a whole, this will impart a cumulative upward trend to the calculated capital-output ratio, and hence a downward bias to measures of total factor productivity. It seems preferable to avoid this pitfall by ignoring capital productivity altogether (particularly as growth accounting studies of centrally planned economies have tended to generate unconvincing results).

8

Yugoslavia: Self-managed Socialism

Introduction

Yugoslavia is well known for its commitment to a much more decentralized form of socialism than that prevailing in eastern Europe. Although the political system is still that of a one-party state, the general atmosphere is considerably more liberal than in the Soviet bloc. The Communist Party itself, by changing its name to the League of Communists, has attempted to create the impression of a more democratic, less rigid and hierarchical organization. In economic life the ideology of central planning has given way to one of self-management, which is characterized as 'direct' socialism as opposed to the 'indirect' or 'state' socialism of the Soviet bloc. Workers' councils have genuine power, and are by no means mere transmission belts for party decisions. In short, Yugoslavia is the one country in Communist-ruled Europe which has deviated significantly from the Soviet model.

Yugoslavia is also unique in Europe in the complexity of its national and regional problems. This is reflected in the division of the country along ethnic lines into six republics and two provinces (provinces are autonomous regions which have a slightly lower status than republics). Economic disparities between regions are as great as in any European country (with the possible exception of Italy, where they are not compounded by ethnic and cultural diversity). In the last two decades ethnic divisions have been accentuated by the devolution of power to republican and lower levels of government, and the growth of nationalism (at the republican rather than the Yugoslav level) has made a significant contribution to current economic problems.

The road to self-management

Yugoslavia was formed as a state only after the First World War. Before that the northern parts – Croatia, Slovenia and Vojvodina – had been under the rule of Austria-Hungary, but Serbia had only thrown off the Turkish yoke and achieved independence in 1878, whilst Macedonia remained under Turkish domination until 1912. Literally, 'Yugoslavia' means the state of the southern Slavs, and more than 80 per cent of the population is ethnically Slav, with small minorities of Hungarians, Germans, Albanians (concentrated mainly in the province of Kosovo, bordering on Albania) and others. However the cultural and religious differences between the various Slav nationalities are extremely important. The two main nationalities are the Serbs and the Croats, who speak what are officially described as two variants of the same language, Serbo-Croat. But the Croats are mainly Catholic, and use the Latin script, whereas the Serbs follow the Eastern Orthodox Church, and use the Cyrillic alphabet. Moreover the northern republics, whose terrain is more hospitable, have a long history of economic integration with central Europe, and are economically much more advanced than the backward mountainous regions of the south. Cultural differences are thus compounded by significant economic disparities.

Developments in the inter-war period had done little to dissolve historical suspicions or to weld a Yugoslav national consciousness. The King, who was a Serb, deliberately fostered Serbian domination of the young state, maintaining a centralized political system in order to limit the power of other nationalities. This fanned the flames of Croat nationalism in particular, and the German occupying forces made good use of this in 1941 by setting up a puppet Croatian state, ruled by local fascists who promptly embarked on a policy of forcible conversion of all inhabitants to Catholicism. This behaviour ensured that wartime occupation and resistance could not have the strong unifying effect on the country that might have been expected. National antagonisms were muted in the resistance movement once it came to be dominated by the Communist Party, which was not identified with any particular nationality and had long advocated a federal state, but the wartime history of Croatia cast a shadow of collaboration over the whole Croat nation.

The resistance played a larger role in the liberation of the country from German rule in Yugoslavia than in any other occupied country. After the capture of Belgrade by the Soviet army, it was quickly handed over to the Yugoslavs. The leaders of the Communist Party of Yugoslavia felt that they had been victorious in a national war of liberation and that they had a popular mandate for revolutionary change. They saw nothing to prevent them from setting up a Stalinist type of socialist state as soon as possible. They were quickly able to eliminate rival political forces, and they lacked the anxieties about their own popularity and the inhibitions about embarrassing Stalin that caused Communists in eastern Europe to tread carefully at this time. The whole of industry was nationalized and a central planning apparatus set up by 1946. A Five-Year Plan was drawn up for the period 1947–51, envisaging very high rates of investment and an expansion of industrial output to five times its pre-war level. The peasantry was subjected to compulsory deliveries of produce, as in the USSR, although a collectivization programme was not initiated until 1949.

In short, the Communist Party of Yugoslavia at this time was impeccably orthodox, and its actions were a foretaste of what eastern Europe was to experience from 1950 to 1953. However there were frictions in its relationship with the Soviet comrades from an early stage. The Yugoslavs were annoyed by Stalin's failure to support their claim to Trieste, and by the inequitable financial arrangements for proposed joint Soviet-Yugoslav companies. They protested when they discovered that the USSR was recruiting Yugoslavs into its intelligence services, obviously for the purpose of spying on the Yugoslav government. Though the Yugoslavs revered Stalin, they were not dependent on him, and were prepared to question his behaviour. This irritated him (after all, the Poles even had a Russian as Minister of Defence), and he began to bring pressure to bear. All Soviet civilian and military advisers were withdrawn in the spring of 1948, and an acrimonious exchange of letters began between the Soviet and Yugoslav Communist Parties. When the Yugoslavs declined to back down, they were excommunicated from the world Communist movement, and an orchestrated campaign began against them. The charge of Titoism figured prominently in the show trials of eastern Europe in 1949–52.

Even more drastic and threatening was the imposition of an economic blockade. The Soviet bloc countries accounted for nearly half of Yugoslav trade in the immediate post-war years, but a dramatic reduction began in the autumn of 1948, and by 1950 trade was virtually nil. The freeze was to last until Khrushchev mended relations with a visit to Belgrade in 1955. These developments destroyed the Yugoslav Five-Year Plan, not only through the direct disruption caused but also because the Yugoslavs had every reason to fear a military attack, and were forced to divert considerable resources to defence.

Pro-Soviet elements in the Yugoslav leadership were purged in 1949, but Tito continued at first to pursue a strictly orthodox course. With time, however, hopes of a reconciliation waned, and it became embarrassing to stick religiously to Stalinist policies whilst being vilified by Stalin. To cultivate an independent, Yugoslav road to socialism began to seem attractive, not only for domestic political reasons, but also to open up the possibilities of assistance from the west. Some time in the spring of 1950 the idea of enterprises being managed by workers' councils was conceived. The law establishing the new arrangements was passed on 26 June 1950.

By this law a workers' council elected biennially by all employees in a secret ballot became, in formal terms, the highest authority within the enterprise. It had the power to appoint the director of the enterprise, but with the important proviso that it could choose only from amongst a shortlist of candidates chosen by a selection committee of which only a third of the members were nominated by the workers' council. The remaining members were chosen by the communal and district authorities, so that political bodies had an effective power of veto over the appointment of enterprise directors (this ruling came into force in December 1953; the position today is essentially the same except that workers' council nominees now make up half of the selection committee). These arrangements made it virtually certain that, if economic and political life had retained its highly centralized character, the role of workers' councils would have been largely formal. Probably in recognition of this, the party leadership began to opt for a much less centralized system of economic management. In April 1951 the Federal Planning Commission was abolished, and in December of that year central planning lost its directive character and ceased to have the force of law. Markets were re-established and prices freed from control to a considerable extent, so that enterprises now had a significant degree of autonomy in deciding their own outputs, inputs and production processes.

In agriculture there was more hesitation in implementing a change of policy. The collectivization programme was initiated and pushed forward with haste in the early stages of the dispute with the USSR, when the Yugoslavs were still anxious to prove their orthodoxy, and collective farms covered about 20 per cent of the arable area by 1950 (Rusinow, 1977). The programme was then halted, but it took another two years for the leadership to accept that the collective farms could not be made popular or economically effective, and to recognize that peasants should be permitted to leave. A law of 1953 allowing this led to the swift dissolution of most of the collectives. An upper limit of ten hectares was then set to private land holdings; this entailed little redistribution of land since the vast bulk of holdings were smaller than this. Although some rather unsuccessful attempts were made in subsequent years to encourage the peasants to form much looser forms of co-operative, Yugoslav agriculture continues to be overwhelmingly dominated by small peasant units.

The ideology of socialism as a 'free association of producers' spread into the political arena, where it brought about a considerable weakening of the power of the federal leadership. Although democratic centralism was retained, internal debate was encouraged and the Executive Committee lost its power to nominate the officers of regional and local party organizations. In order to emphasize the democratic nature of these changes, the party apparatus was disentangled from that of the hierarchical state bureaucracy, and the new name 'League of Communists of Yugoslavia' was adopted.

With the abolition of directive planning, the authorities were forced to develop other means to secure their objectives. Primary amongst these was the control of investment. Enterprises had very little autonomy in this area before 1965. In the years 1960–3, 60 per cent of investment was financed by the state, 35 per cent from enterprise funds and only 5 per cent by bank credits (Prout, 1985, Annex 6). Funds for state investment were raised through a variety of taxes on profits and a 6 per cent rental charge on capital assets. The state also took a direct interest in the distribution of the enterprise's net income. The distinction between wages and profits was maintained, and enterprises were not permitted to raise wages on their own initiative. Net profits had to be shared with the local commune, which had the right to determine its own share. Thus the net profit remaining to the enterprise was very much a residual, and annual profit shares received by workers were typically of the order of one month's wages, although they could be much larger (Rusinow, 1977, p. 66). In 1958 the formal distinction between wages and profits was abolished, but the practical significance of this was deliberately limited by strict rules concerning the distribution of enterprise net income. Initially, all banks were merged into the National Bank, which was thus in a strong position to monitor enterprise transactions. But this was soon reckoned to be unnecessary and unsatisfactory, and communal banks were set up, under the control of local government.

This system was initially successful in generating a high rate of investment and of economic growth. The balance of trade was in continuous deficit, but in the 1950s this was covered by western aid. However, there was increasing doubt about the rationality of many investments. Local communes used their right to establish their own share of enterprise profits to finance new factories in their area, in order to generate employment and future tax revenue, without great concern for considerations of profitability. These projects soon acquired the derogatory name of 'political factories'. Moreover an increasing degree of central control over prices, together with local government's power of veto over the appointment of enterprise directors and the high degree of redistribution of profits, reduced the element of genuine competition in the market place and created an environment of soft budget constraints.

Despite the high rate of growth, considerable concern began to be expressed about economic performance, particularly when the trade deficit began to widen alarmingly in 1959. In the years 1960–62 economic growth was significantly slower than before, and unemployment began to appear, whilst a sizeable devaluation of the dinar in 1961 set off a bout of inflation. In these circumstances a considerable movement began, initially amongst economists but subsequently with strong support from the party leaderships in the northern republics, for a liberalization of the self-management system, giving enterprises much greater say over investment decisions. This campaign appealed especially to the richer regions, where it was interpreted as a demand for a reduction in the transfer of resources to the poorer areas. For the same reason, these proposals were received with suspicion in the south, and were strongly opposed by the Serbian leadership, which was of a centralist persuasion. However the Serbs made the tactical mistake of allowing their opposition to become at least partially identified with pressure for a 'uniform Yugoslav socialist culture', about which noises were being made at the time, and this alienated the smaller southern republics, who feared a revival of pre-war Serbian chauvinism. Thus, after a prolonged struggle, a reform was enacted in 1965 which not only represented a considerable reduction of state control over enterprises but also greatly weakened the powers of the federal government – a reflection of the Yugoslav propensity to identify federal organizations with domination by other ethnic groups.

Although, in the years after 1965 as before, there have been frequent changes to the rules of the game, that year marks a decisive moment in the history of Yugoslav self-management because enterprises acquired much greater freedom to decide their own investments, and this reform has not been significantly reversed in subsequent years. This is reflected in the figures for investment finance: by the late 1960s less than 10 per cent of investment was being financed out of tax revenue, with bank credit and enterprises' own savings each contributing about half of the remaining 90 per cent. The process of liberalization had in fact begun in early 1961, when government control over the distribution of enterprise net income was abolished. This was accompanied by a devaluation, abolition of the multiple exchange rate system (though this was to reappear fairly swiftly) and the transfer of the commercial banking functions of the National Bank to the communal banks and to three specialized banks which had been set up in the mid-1950s. The combined effect of these changes was to create severe overheating in the economy. Enterprises used their new autonomy to increase wages, taking out bank loans to maintain capital investments, and taking advantage of the devaluation to raise prices. The government reacted with emergency deflationary measures, which caused a severe reduction in the growth rate. A similar pattern of overheating followed by deflation recurred in 1964–5. Nevertheless, despite these unpromising developments, the political struggle was won by the advocates of decentralization.

An immediate effect of this was the generalization of the principle of self-management to all areas of the economy except government administration and the military. The 'non-productive sector' (health, education and other social services) was taken out of the government budget and organized into self-managing 'communities of interest'. The difference between communities of interest and ordinary enterprises is that a substantial part of the income of the former comes from contributions rather than user charges or sales. In recognition of this, contributing enterprises were given equal weight in the management of the communities with the employees. The intention was that in the absence of normal market constraints on self-management, the users would exert direct influence over the quantity and quality of services provided through participation in the management committee. However, there is a strong suspicion that this system tends to allow the employees of communities of interest to write their own budgets, since the representatives of contributing enterprises lack sufficient specialist knowledge to oppose them and are less able to act as a coherent force on the management committee (Lydall, 1984, pp. 123–6).

For other enterprises, the main effect of the 1965 changes was to confirm their new autonomy, but they also benefited from a reduction in the fiscal burden and a greater degree of influence over the banks. The interest charge on capital was reduced in three steps, reaching zero in 1971, and the tax system was overhauled with the ultimate intention of reducing the state's share of enterprise net income from 49 to 29 per cent (Rusinow, 1977, p. 177). From the point of view of the federal government, this meant a very considerable reduction in its economic powers, which was matched by a devolution of its political power in a series of amendments to the constitution. Federal responsibilities were now confined to defence, pensions, foreign debt and the Fund for the Development of Underdeveloped Regions, which now became the sole vehicle of regional policy. The Banking and Credit Law which came into force in 1966 transferred control of banks from government bodies to enterprises. In the spirit of de-bureaucratization, banks were regarded as a kind of 'financial community of interest', except that the investing enterprises were more powerful in this case relative to the employees. Government bodies were allowed to put up capital for a bank in conjunction with enterprises, but could never collectively control more than 20 per cent of the votes (Prout, 1985, p. 43). This reform had the important effect of putting banks under the control of their chief debtors – a point to which I shall return. For the first time private peasants were permitted to borrow from banks and purchase farm machinery.

The dramatic weakening of federal power had far-reaching political effects, creating the illusion amongst regional party leaderships that they were secure in their fiefs and more or less immune from dismissal by the national leaders. This feeling was reinforced by the dismissal in 1966 of Ranković, Organizational Secretary of the LCY for twenty years, after which control of League appointments passed entirely into the control of republican organs. Republican politicians began to flirt with nationalist agitators, particularly but by no means exclusively in Croatia, and for the first time since 1945 the national question forced itself to the surface of political life. The amendments to the constitution had given the republics an effective power of veto on many issues. Almost every question came to be viewed in ethnic terms. The resurgence of nationalism was only stemmed in 1971, when it was reaching crisis proportions, by decisive action by Tito against sections of the Croatian leadership. Though this averted the immediate danger, it did not reverse the tendency towards fragmentation of the federation as an economic unit initiated by the reforms, and ethnic divisions continue to smoulder very close to the surface of political life.

Another new and significant feature of the 1960s was the emergence of a significant problem of unemployment, which was, however, greatly alleviated by emigration of workers to parts of western Europe, above all West Germany. By 1970 Yugoslavs working abroad numbered more than a million, and their remittances helped to service a continuing visible trade deficit.

In the early 1970s there were some further changes which were intended to consolidate the self-management system. By a reform of 1974 the fundamental productive unit ceased to be the enterprise, which was replaced in this role by the 'basic organization of associated labour' (BOAL). Enterprises were renamed 'work organizations of associated labour' and could consist of more than one BOAL, although in fact only about a quarter of them had split in this way by 1980 (Lydall, 1984, p. 93). In this case the constitutent BOALs make 'self-management agreements' to work together as enterprises, but might later agree to separate. A BOAL must have a marketable output of its own; in effect, a BOAL can be thought of as a division of an enterprise which could potentially split off to form a separate entity. The object of this legislation was, where possible, to reduce the size of self-management units in order to minimize the danger of bureaucratization. At the same time local government was given the right to extend the community of interest system to infrastructure services, such as power and transport.

The 1974 Constitution also consolidated the control of enterprises and BOALs over the banks. Government bodies were now no longer permitted to be bank shareholders, and control of the credit committees, which decided the banks' loan policy, passed from the employees to the shareholders (Rusinow, 1977, p. 329).

The desire to make self-management the underlying principle of all social life was apparent throughout the 1974 Constitution. Planning was now styled 'self-management social planning', and the intention was that all bodies should somehow agree amongst themselves to make consistent plans that would fit into the framework of the federal Five-Year Plan. Since the resulting plans are not enforceable, it is unlikely that this process really amounts to much more than a rather time-consuming exchange of information (Lydall, 1984, pp. 137–49).

On the political side, communes were renamed 'socio-political communities' and given wide powers of revenue-raising, to emphasize their independence from higher levels of government. In general, communes now have much larger powers than local governments typically do in other countries.

A change of fundamental importance was the replacement of direct elections to legislative bodies, even down to the communal level, by a delegate system. At the federal level, one chamber is elected directly by the assemblies of communes in each republic or province, but the other (the Chamber of Republics and Provinces) is elected by a joint session of the chambers of the relevant republic or province. This system means that members of the federal legislature act very much as delegates of their region, particularly in the Chamber of Republics and Provinces, which has exclusive power over major economic issues. Since the practice in this Chamber is to carry a measure only if it secures unanimous support, this provision effectively gives each region a power of veto over economic policy. 'In fact, the country entered a phase in which there was no effective mechanism to bring about macroeconomic structural adjustments' (UNECE, 1984/5, p. 84). The Constitution of 1974 thereby confirmed the fundamental weakness of federal bodies in economic matters that had been evident since 1965, and reinforced the tendency to regional fragmentation.

With the Constitution of 1974 the principle of self-management was taken about as far as it was possible to do so. The subsequent years have seen some dramatic economic developments, but institutional arrangements have undergone relatively little fundamental alteration (despite a continuous stream of minor amendments).

The theory of the labour-managed enterprise

A very considerable literature has grown up over the last three decades on the theory of the labour-managed enterprise. A systematic review of this literature is not possible here, and I shall refer only to its main results. Self-management may take many forms, and it is important to be clear about the ideological preconceptions which have moulded the Yugoslav version. In Yugoslavia, self-management is viewed as a more immediate and direct form of socialism than the 'state socialism' of the USSR. In terms of the Marxist theory of the state, the Yugoslavs argue that the 'withering away of the state' projected by Marx for the classless utopia of communism, must begin immediately, and the system of self-management is a practical expression of this belief. It is emphatically *not* the intention to make some kind of compromise with capitalism, nor to reproduce any element of capitalist exploitation under another guise; for this reason private sector activities have only been tolerated with some reluctance, as we shall see later.

As far as the self-managed enterprise is concerned, this means that no fundamental distinctions can be made between employees with respect to management rights. An enterprise cannot hire additional workers, even temporarily, on a purely contractual basis, without giving these workers the same rights as other employees; nor can workers buy and sell entitlements to profit shares. Legally, in fact, the enterprise is still owned by the state, and the employees only have rights of use over its assets, not rights of ownership. The workers are therefore not shareholders; they simply enjoy the benefits equivalent to shareholding so long as they remain employed by the enterprise.

Since the state now makes no rental charge on capital assets, employees of social sector enterprises effectively enjoy windfall gains from free use of these assets. This will tend to bias enterprise decisions towards consumption of net income in many circumstances, for instance where there is a high turnover of labour, where a large proportion of the workforce is approaching retiring age, or where employees strongly prefer present over future consumption. Because the government is aware of this and wishes to maintain a high rate of investment, it has always retained some power to influence the division of enterprise income. Indeed the relative ineffectiveness of available fiscal and monetary policy instruments has rendered this a prime instrument of demand management in recent years. An unavoidable effect of a self-management system in which enterprises have genuine choice over the division of income is that workers in different enterprises will get very different rewards for the same work. To minimize the social consequences of this the government has exerted some pressure on enterprises with relatively high value added per worker to save more. In the long run, this policy is likely to exacerbate regional differences if pursued systematically, as the richer enterprises which are thereby forced to invest at a higher rate tend to be in the richer regions.

The appearance of unemployment in Yugoslavia, on a scale and with a time pattern not dissimilar to that of western Europe, has been linked by many observers to the operation of self-management. The argument runs as follows. New workers automatically acquire the same profits share and security of tenure as existing workers in the same job category. This has a number of consequences. An increase in demand which is feared to be only temporary is unlikely to be met by additional hirings, because the new workers cannot be dismissed if demand falls back to its original level, and their presence would then depress the net income of existing employees. Whereas the capitalist firm maximizes profits, the labour-managed firm will maximize net income per (current) employee. An expansion of employment which increases net income in less than the same proportion will seem unattractive to the labour-managed firm, and it can be shown that in general the labour-managed firm will choose more capital-intensive techniques of production than a capitalist firm faced with the same technological possibilities. The reason is that additional labour effectively costs more to the labour-managed firm, since it receives a share of the profits as well as a wage. The combined effect of the bias towards capital intensity and the security of tenure of new workers is to inhibit the growth of employment.

In reality, it does not appear to be necessary to prove that the Yugoslav system generates *more* unemployment than a comparable capitalist economy, since the figures do not support such an assertion (see table 8.1). It is sufficient to show that unemployment rates will be similar to those under capitalism, because the Yugoslav system does not generate the excess demand for labour apparent in eastern Europe. In fact there *are* political pressures on enterprises from government bodies in Yugoslavia to take on more labour and thus to reduce the burden of unemployment; the primary effect of the self-management system is probably to render enterprises strongly resistant to these pressures, because excess labour has a clear cost to existing employees. In circumstances where the political anxieties about unemployment do not conflict with enterprise interests, as for example when an enterprise is making a loss and is threatened with bankruptcy, then the bias of the system is very much towards employment protection. An enterprise in trouble is helped out with loans, or if its difficulties persist, it may be merged into another enterprise in the same district. In short, there is a strong aversion to

Table 8.1 Unemployment in south European countries in 1986

Country	*Percentage of labour force unemployed*
Greece	9.0
Portugal	10.3
Spain	21.5
Turkey	17.3
Yugoslavia	14.3

Note: a substantial proportion (perhaps of the order of 40 per cent, although the exact figure is highly uncertain) of those registered as unemployed in Yugoslavia would not qualify according to definitions used elsewhere.
Source: UNECE (1986/7), p. 58

penalizing employees of loss-making enterprises by closing them down (bankruptcies are comparatively rare) or even by substantial cuts in their net income – a situation reminiscent of eastern Europe, where soft budget constraints are the norm (I shall return to this point).

Enterprises are not confined to their historical sphere of operation, and are free to move into markets which they expect to generate high net income. Thus enterprises can expect to face competition from new entrants, and in theory this process should lead to an equalization of net incomes per worker between industries. In the context of the tendency towards regional fragmentation of the economy, however, this process is inhibited by the lack of a unified Yugoslav market, and new entry often takes the form of import-substituting investment encouraged by republics or communes, where 'imports' in this case are taken to mean goods produced outside the immediate area. By the early 1980s there were five car factories producing five different makes of car, and five oil refineries operating at half-capacity, with two more in the course of construction (OECD, 1982). Competition from imports from abroad is less restricted than in the rest of eastern Europe, but there is still much protection of domestic producers, and imports continue to represent a rather small proportion of national income.

It is also possible for enterprises to invest in one another, for an agreed rate of return or share of profits. In theory, this provision means that enterprises earning high rates of return could attract capital from others, though the investing enterprise cannot acquire management rights nor sell its holding, which creates an understandable reluctance to sink funds in such investments. According to OECD (1987), this is in fact less of a deterrent than the possibility of the enterprise which receives the funds dissolving itself into its constituent BOALs.

A further potential source of competition is the creation of new co-operatives and private sector enterprises. In 1965, it became permissible for groups of individuals to set up their own self-management enterprises using their own capital, on which they were entitled to receive interest. The main incentive to set up such an organization was not the interest thus received, but rather the net income expected to be earned as a member of a collective which was anticipated to be highly profitable. After a sustained press campaign against the high incomes gained in these new enterprises, the rules were changed in 1969 so that a local government committee would undertake the hiring of the workers in such collectives, and this, together with a number of other restrictions, effectively killed off this kind of citizen-created enterprise (Prout, 1985, pp. 176–7).

The private sector remains important in Yugoslavia, employing about a third of the active labour force in 1980, compared with 60 per cent in 1960. The bulk of private sector activity is in agriculture, where about 85 per cent of the land is in private hands, and it is the shrinkage of employment in this sector which accounts for the steady fall in the relative significance of the private sector. Elsewhere in the economy, private sector enterprises are mostly concentrated in construction, tourism, catering, transport and handicrafts (Lydall, 1984, ch. 13). Until 1965, private peasants continued to be discriminated against quite severely, despite the abandonment of the collectivization campaign, because it was still hoped to encourage the development of looser forms of co-operatives in agriculture. After 1965 they were permitted to obtain loans, but often at a higher rate of interest than social sector enterprises. The legal limit on land holdings of ten hectares has been raised only for mountain areas, and certainly inhibits the development of the agricultural sector. As in Poland, hostile official attitudes have kept agricultural output below potential, and this grudging acceptance of the private peasant has had poorer results than the Hungarian approach of flexible collectivization.

The general rule is that private enterprises are allowed to employ about five persons (depending on republic) over and above family labour, so that such enterprises are bound to remain small. As Prout (1985, p. 143) points out, the 1974 Constitution gives the authorities power to convert 'that part of income which is the result of the surplus labour of workers' employed in private enterprise into social property, a provision which could be invoked at any time to deprive the private sector of most of its assets.

Economic performance up to 1979

Any assessment of Yugoslav economic performance must take account of the dramatic differences between the periods before and after 1979. Up to 1979 performance appeared relatively good, though with some weak-

Table 8.2 The economic development of Yugoslavia 1970–86

	Average 1970–8	*1979*	*% change over previous year 1980*	*1981*	*1982*	*1983*	*1984*	*1985*	*1986*
Gross social product (GSP)	6.1	7.0	2.3	1.5	0.5	−1.0	2.0	0.5	3.6
GSP per employee	1.8	2.7	−0.9	−1.4	−1.8	−3.0	−0.1	−2.0	0.6
Private consumption	6.5	5.6	0.7	−1.0	−0.1	−1.7	−1.0	–	3.5
Public consumption	6.4	4.5	−1.0	−4.8	−0.7	−5.1	−0.2	−0.3	4.6
Gross fixed investment	8.8	6.4	−5.9	−9.8	−5.5	−9.7	−9.6	−4.0	1.0
Consumer prices	16.4	20.3	31.0	42.1	31.5	40.8	53.4	74.0	90.0
Investment/GSP (%)	32.8	38.4	35.1	31.0	29.2	25.3	23.1	22.8	22.2
Unemployment (%)	9.3	11.9	11.9	11.9	12.4	12.8	13.3	13.8	14.3
Current account balance ($ million)	−429	−3665	−2316	−961	−475	275	504	800	1000

Sources: UNECE (1986/7), Appendix A
OECD *Economic Survey of Yugoslavia* (various years), Table A

nesses; in the 1980s the picture is one of stagnation, chronic inflation and an accumulation of difficulties. Clearly the change did not come overnight, and we shall find that beneath the apparently strong growth performance of the 1970s there were already warnings of deterioration.

In the early period, Yugoslavia experienced strong growth of output, and there is no evidence of exaggeration in the official figures. Labour productivity grew at 5.4 per cent per annum between 1950 and 1967. This figure is slightly above the average for southern Europe over this period, and higher than that achieved by any west European country (UNECE, 1971, Part I, Table 1.8). In the 1970s output continued to grow fast, but employment growth accelerated, so that from 1969 to 1979 output per employee grew at an average rate of less than 2 per cent per annum (see table 8.2). Moreover an unusually large proportion of resources was devoted to investment. Gross fixed investment averaged 28 per cent of GDP from 1965 to 1979, compared with 18–24 per cent for Greece, Portugal, Spain and Turkey, and yet these countries all achieved very much the same rate of growth of output as Yugoslavia over this period (OECD, 1981). This suggests a persistent problem of inefficiency in Yugoslav investment, which has been to some extent disguised by its high volume (though public awareness of it is indicated by frequent allusion to 'political factories').

Nevertheless, in the course of three decades, Yugoslavia was transformed from an overwhelmingly agrarian economy into a significant producer and exporter of manufactures, worthy of inclusion in the list of 'newly industrializing countries'. In 1950, private sector agriculture accounted for 70 per cent of all employment; by the 1980s it had fallen to 30 per cent. By 1980, about 80 per cent of exports consisted of finished manufactures, semi-manufactures and chemicals, whereas in the pre-war period exports had been dominated by raw materials. Since 1975 the centrally planned economies (the CMEA countries plus China and Albania) have absorbed 45–50 per cent of Yugoslavia's exports, but provided only about 30 per cent of its imports. This discrepancy reflects the fact that Yugoslavia's trade with centrally planned economies is approximately balanced, whereas it has been running a sizeable trade deficit with market economies.

As already mentioned, there is an officially acknowledged problem of unemployment in Yugoslavia, and unemployment benefits are available to those who have made the relevant social insurance contributions. In the boom period in western Europe from 1965 to 1973, there was amazingly rapid emigration of workers, particularly to West Germany. At their peak in 1973 emigrant workers accounted for 12 per cent of the Yugoslav labour force, compared with 2 per cent in 1965. Not surprisingly, this alleviated the potential problem of domestic unemployment, although the registered unemployment rate still rose from 2.7 per cent in 1965 to 4.2 per cent in 1973. After 1973 labour market conditions deteriorated sharply in western Europe, and by 1980 emigrants had shrunk to 8.2 per cent of the labour force, with unemployment reaching 8.4 per cent. Thus in this period strong domestic growth created employment for the domestic increase in the labour force, but could not absorb the reflux of emigrants. By 1986 registered unemployment had reached 14.3 per cent of the labour force (though this included many persons who may already have had jobs outside the social sector). The increase in unemployment from 1980 to 1986 was surprisingly small considering the sharp reduction in the growth rate of output (to virtually zero); the explanation is that employment continued to grow quite rapidly, and labour productivity has fallen steadily since 1979. It must be presumed that there is now substantial underemployment in the social sector, and that the unemployment figures will not respond much to increases in output until this is absorbed.

Yugoslavia has had a poor, and indeed steadily deteriorating, record of inflation since the beginnings of the self-management era. Even in the 1950s, price increases averaged 5 per cent annually, rather above the typical west European rate. In the 1960s the rate of inflation averaged 12 per cent per annum, though with some fluctuation. Between 1969 and 1979 the average annual rate was 17 per cent. In the 1980s inflation has become chronic, accelerating in every year but one and exceeding 100 per cent in 1987. The factors behind the recent acceleration are discussed in the next section.

The primary cause of the inflationary problem is the combination of persistently strong demand conditions with a relatively protected market. Prices have risen particularly strongly after devaluations of the currency. In capitalist economies wages do not usually adjust immediately to a rise in import prices, and since pricing is mainly cost-based (outside the primary producing sector), devaluation tends to result in a fall in domestic prices relative to foreign prices. In the self-management system, there are no wage costs, and enterprises tend to adjust their prices rather rapidly to the increased cost of imported products. This is encouraged by the barriers to competition in Yugoslavia; although in principle Yugoslavia is supposed to constitute one unified market, in practice significant barriers to trade have grown up between republics, which has created a proliferation of oligopolistic situations. Thus there is little to stop enterprises rapidly readjusting domestic prices to compensate for a devaluation.

The institutional structure of the Yugoslav economy probably induces a smaller degree of political resistance to inflation than elsewhere. The self-management system in the social sector amounts effectively to full indexation of wages, at least in relation to the prices of the enterprise's own products. This is likely to divert concern from the *absolute* to the *relative* rate of inflation. Whilst every self-management unit might prefer a non-inflationary environment, in a situation where inflation already exists it will agitate to be able to raise its *own* prices as fast as possible. In the absence of a strong anti-inflationary policy from the authorities, this pressure can easily kindle a rapid acceleration of inflation. As we shall see later, the devolution of price setting to the republics in 1980 seems to have initiated a mechanism of this kind, with republics hoping, by increasing their own rate of inflation, to make terms of trade gains against others.

Lydall (1984, ch. 9) has summarized the evidence on income distribution in Yugoslavia. Earnings of full-time workers in the social sector display about the same degree of inequality as in other countries, although the Yugoslav data are not exactly comparable. It seems likely, however (and it is widely believed in Yugoslavia), that the variation between enterprises in net income per worker creates a relatively wide dispersion of rates of remuneration for the same work across the economy, whereas within a given enterprise the dispersion of incomes according to skill is relatively low. Thus *intra*-skill pay dispersion is relatively high and *inter*-skill dispersion rather low, and it can happen that a highly skilled worker in one enterprise is less well paid than an unskilled worker in another.

The distribution of earnings by household is more equal than in capitalist countries at a similar stage of development, but slightly more unequal than in the most advanced capitalist countries. When households are ranked by per capita income, according to the east European practice, the Yugoslav distribution comes out significantly more unequal than eastern Europe. One reason for this may be the low incomes earned in the agricultural sector. In countries with collectivized agriculture, there has been some effort in recent decades to improve the relative position of agricultural workers, whereas in Yugoslavia the ten hectare limit on landholdings and the official reluctance to extend social services to private peasants has kept agricultural earnings relatively low. A more important reason, however, is the apparent failure of regional policy to close the wide income gap between regions. In 1978, the per capita resources of the average Slovenian household were more than 50 per cent above the national average, whilst the average household in Kosovo was 55 per cent below the national average and in Macedonia 28 per cent below (Lydall, 1984, Table 9.2). Data from the censuses of 1953 and 1971 show a widening of the regional dispersion, with labour productivity and per capita incomes increasing faster in the richer republics than in the poorer ones. Regional policy was successful in pumping investment resources into the poorer areas, bringing their capital–labour ratios up to the level of the richer republics, but the poorer republics still lost ground because their capital–output ratios were higher (Prout, 1985, p. 145). Regional policy has therefore failed in its prime objective, to reduce income differentials between rich and poor republics. This has exacerbated ethnic tensions, leaving the inhabitants of the poorer regions disgruntled whilst those of the richer regions resent the cost of apparently fruitless regional development schemes.

It has already been mentioned that high taxation of profits and government control of investment funds created an environment of soft budget constraints in the 1950s. To what extent were budget constraints hardened by the 'de-étatization' of 1965? As it turns out, not very much. Loss-making enterprises (of which there are many) are rescued from bankruptcy by loans from the banks, or else they simply force suppliers to extend credit by failing to pay their bills. Politically, the government is unwilling to countenance bankruptcies of social sector enterprises, so most of the time monetary policy is lax enough for enterprises to obtain bank credit. If macroeconomic circumstances lead to the imposition of a tight monetary policy, trade credit starts to replace bank loans. This phenomenon is very evident in the 1980s. Banks lend money to loss-making enterprises because, since 1965, enterprises have been the main shareholders in their local banks; moreover if local, regional and national government bodies are unwilling to see enterprises go bankrupt and are prepared to guarantee their debts, the risk involved in such lending is not very great either.

In the Yugoslav context, official aversion to bankruptcies in the social sector need not be of great significance if workers in loss-making enterprises are severely penalized. If workers only received the incomes that enterprises could afford to pay, and enterprises were forbidden to run at a loss, then poor performance would be immediately reflected in workers' remuneration. Employees would then exert pressure on management through the workers' council, and if that was ineffective they would seek work elsewhere. However employees are not effectively penalized in this way, and enterprises are permitted to pay out more in net incomes than they earn in net revenue. Laura Tyson (1977) has described this as the 'worker-manager' view of self-management, where the workers other than the director and top managerial staff have 'an inalienable right to a steady income and a steady job', in contrast to the 'pure-co-operative' view, where all members of an enterprise are 'collectively responsible for enterprise decisions and therefore collectively accountable for the financial consequences of those decisions'. She goes on to show how the Yugoslav commitment to the former view has resulted in the development of a variety of sanctions against persistently loss-making enterprises, all of which protect the incomes of workers in that enterprise. Possible sanctions include the temporary installation of a director chosen by the creditors, placing the enterprise under temporary state management, requiring it to present plans to local government for eliminating its debts, and the partial blocking of its current account. But so long as employees' incomes are protected, they are under no pressure to improve performance or to move to areas of the economy where their efforts would be more productive. Thus budget constraints are soft, and structural and organizational inefficiencies are perpetuated.

The 1980s: foreign indebtedness and stagnation

As in eastern Europe, the macroeconomic effect of soft budget constraints was not very evident in the 1950s and 1960s, when the speedy transfer of labour out of agriculture in conjunction with a high rate of investment could sustain strong growth. However, when oil prices rose very sharply and the long boom in the west came to an end in 1974, the repercussions were immediately felt in Yugoslavia. A huge deficit opened up in the current account of the balance of payments. Yugoslavia suffered a terms of trade loss of 65 per cent with market economies in the period 1974–6, which was compounded by a fall in the market share of its exports to the now slower-growing western markets that was equivalent to a 24 per cent cut in export revenues (Balassa and Tyson, 1986). In fact this loss of market share had been occurring for at least a decade, but before 1974 it had been obscured by the buoyancy of invisible earnings (principally workers' remittances and tourism). The much slower growth of these invisible earnings after 1974 was a further cause of deterioration in the current account. At first the authorities' policy was to maintain a high rate of investment and growth, keeping nominal interest rates low and real interest rates negative, whilst using additional incentives to exports and import substitution to close the payments gap. Nevertheless within a few years a considerable foreign debt was built up. But in 1979 this strategy became unsustainable for a number of reasons: a further round of oil price increases, the rapid increase in the foreign debt and in the interest rates payable on it, and a renewed weakening of export markets. The government was forced to introduce restrictive measures. In 1980 investment was cut back, public expenditure reduced, and enterprises were ordered to distribute a lower proportion of value added than in the previous year.

As can be seen from table 8.2, this marked the beginning of a prolonged period of austerity in which growth virtually came to a halt. Consumers' expenditure was fairly well maintained, but was still less in 1985 than it had been in 1979, whilst public consumption and especially investment declined very rapidly. Gross fixed capital formation fell from nearly 40 per cent of gross social product in 1978 to 22 per cent in 1986. This policy has certainly succeeded in rectifying the current account, which has improved in every year since 1979 and has been in surplus since 1983; and the foreign debt has been stabilized at about $20 billion. In 1986 the fall in oil prices permitted the resumption of import growth, and labour productivity actually increased for the first time since 1979.

Nevertheless it is difficult to assess the economic situation of Yugoslavia at the end of the 1980s as other than bleak – indeed significantly bleaker than when the crisis first broke in 1979. A balance of trade gap amounting to 10 per cent of gross social product has been more or less closed, but at the expense of a collapse of investment (admittedly from an extremely high level), a sustained fall in labour productivity and virtually no growth in output. The foreign debt is smaller in real terms, and not seriously out of line with that of other south European countries as a percentage of export receipts, but still represents a significant burden. Labour productivity fell by no less than 9 per cent between 1979 and 1985, and in 1986 was still below its 1974 level. As Balassa and

Tyson (1986) have noted, the economic history of Yugoslavia since 1973 invites comparison with Hungary. In both countries policy remained growth-oriented after the first oil shock, at the expense of a rapid increase in foreign indebtedness. The advent of the second oil shock forced both to bring in a stabilization programme, after which both seem to have become locked into a downward spiral. Domestic demand was sharply curtailed, with investment taking the brunt of the reduction and consumption being largely protected, but both economies were revealed to have little resilience to import restrictions, and could not easily evolve new import-saving techniques. This lack of adaptability is almost certainly attributable in both cases to the softness of budget constraints, which removes the pressure on enterprises and individuals to alter their old patterns of behaviour.

Nowhere is the failure of Yugoslav economic policy in recent years more apparent than in the field of price stability. As may be seen from table 8.2, the rate of inflation, which was reasonably stable at 10–20 per cent per annum up to 1979, has undergone a very sharp acceleration in the 1980s, reaching a rate of 135 per cent in 1987. In 1980 there was a substantial devolution of price control from the federal to the republican, provincial and communal authorities associated with the establishment of 'communities for prices'. These consist of representatives of producers, chambers of commerce and the appropriate level of government. As previously mentioned, this measure created an incentive to increase local prices so as to make resource gains *vis-à-vis* the rest of the country, and is probably the main cause of the rapid acceleration of inflation. Although there has been a series of temporary price freezes, their effect has been speedily reversed in subsequent periods of relaxation of the controls.

The federal authorities rely to a considerable degree on monetary policy to control inflation. However, their target variable, M1 (notes and coin plus dinar cheque accounts) represents only a fraction of the liquid resources available. Real M1 fell by a half between 1979 and 1985, but this did not represent a genuine squeeze on the liquidity of either households or enterprises. As in previous monetary squeezes, trade credit expanded to fill the gap, so that by 1985 its real value was 50 per cent greater than in 1979 (OECD, 1987, p. 56). Households have long had the option of holding foreign currency bank accounts earning positive real rates of interest, and since dinar real interest rates remain negative despite considerable increases in nominal rates since 1980, there has been a steady flight into foreign currency over the years, as table 8.3 demonstrates. The fall in real M1 reflects economic agents' flight from the dinar – the classic response to a hyper-inflationary situation – and is not an

Table 8.3 Foreign currency assets held by Yugoslav households 1970–85

Year	*Percentage of total household financial assets held in foreign currencies*
1970	18.4
1975	33.6
1980	45.2
1985	58.0

Source: OECD *Economic Survey of Yugoslavia* (1987), Table 15, p. 36

indication of exceptional monetary tightness. It is not surprising, therefore, that the authorities have so far failed in their declared objective of making real interest rates positive.

Although steps have recently been taken, such as a new banking law passed in 1985, which represent a recognition that the financial environment has been over-indulgent, it is difficult to imagine that major reforms will follow. The devolution of political power encourages patronage of local enterprises by government bodies which are not required and have no incentive to take a pan-Yugoslav view, while ethnic jealousies and tensions create enormous difficulties in bringing about fundamental changes of policy, whose full consequences cannot be accurately foreseen. No republican or provincial party leadership is willing to take the risk that their region may turn out to be major losers from change. In the absence of direct elections and with federal legislative bodies chosen at republican and provincial level, the federal government is essentially the prisoner of the republics and provinces, and is not in a position to initiate major measures without their agreement. This is the principal reason for believing that Yugoslavia's economic prospects are significantly worse than those for other south European countries. The problems are already apparent in the record of growth in the post-1973 period. Whereas elsewhere in southern Europe labour productivity has continued to grow at more than two per cent per annum, slightly above the west European average, in Yugoslavia it has not grown at all (see table 7.4). Over a fifteen-year period, this amounts to a relative drop of 30 per cent.

Conclusions

After the break with Stalin and the adoption of the ideology of self-management, the Yugoslav economy initially took a form which bore some resemblance to that of Hungary under the New Economic Mechanism, though with some institutional differences. The traditional mechanisms of central planning had been dismantled, and elements of a market system appeared; but these were not predominant and state bodies remained the determining force in economic development, particularly with regard to investment. The reforms of the early 1960s marked a decisive step towards what Hungarian economists would call a 'regulated market system'. The power of the federal government was greatly weakened, both formally through amendments to the constitution and informally through a loss of control over party appointments in the republics and provinces. The National Bank of Yugoslavia lost its remaining supervisory functions over enterprises, effectively becoming a central bank with responsibilities similar to that of a market economy. Foreign trade was liberalized and a uniform exchange rate established, though restrictions on imports continued in force to varying degrees, depending on the balance of payments situation.

The attempt to create a form of market socialism with genuine workers' control over enterprises excited considerable international interest. However it fairly soon became apparent that the practice did not quite live up to the theory. Although the federal government was required to ensure the unity of the Yugoslav market, it no longer had the power to enforce the rules of the game. Lower levels of government, at the republican/provincial and communal levels, used their enhanced powers to subsidize investment projects which they considered desirable, to protect enterprises in their area from bankruptcy and generally to advance the interests of their locality as against others, even if this built up the barriers to competition. The result has been considerable fragmentation of the Yugoslav market – according to figures cited in OECD (1984), inter-regional trade fell from 27.4 to 22.2 per cent of the total between 1970 and 1980 – and a paternalistic environment in which enterprises expect support from local government bodies when threatened with serious difficulties. Moreover, workers' incomes are heavily protected from the consequences of enterprise losses. In short, enterprises and their employees do not face the hard budget constraints that one might expect in a market environment. The political basis of this development is the conception of self-management as an advanced form of socialism rather than as an economic device designed to create an incentive to effort. As Tyson (1977) has pointed out, the belief that workers should be insured against loss and not suffer for the failures of enterprise management is well entrenched. The system is different from eastern Europe in that some people (private peasants, the unemployed) are effectively outside this network of economic security, but once a foothold in the social sector has been obtained, security of income and employment is virtually guaranteed. The willingness to subsidize inefficiency, the lack of financial discipline and the softness of enterprise budget constraints are now being fully reflected in macroeconomic performance, with labour productivity falling in the social sector and manufacturing exports failing to maintain their share of western markets. In these circumstances, as in eastern Europe, deflation tends to result in stagnation without structural adjustment. The pressure to make such adjustments is lacking, and sharp cutbacks in investment remove the engine of growth. Though this dilemma is increasingly apparent to Yugoslav policy-makers, the political system inhibits decisive action on even the most pressing problems, as the failure of the republics to agree on an effective anti-inflationary policy amply demonstrates.

9

Assessment

Supporters of socialism have consistently believed that it is a 'higher' mode of production than capitalism. Opponents have generally based their case on the alleged deterioration in economic performance that takes place once the incentives provided by greed and ambition are stunted by an egalitarian ideology and public ownership of the means of production. How much can we learn about these issues from the countries examined in this book?

It is evident that the social systems of the USSR and eastern Europe do not represent a very wide spectrum of types of socialism. Variety is constrained primarily by the comparative homogeneity of their political structure, which is modelled on that developed in the USSR in the years after the October revolution. Any other political parties that continue to exist are completely subordinate to the Communist Party, which is the only effective political body, whose 'leading role' is universally acknowledged. At elections, the voters frequently have no choice of candidates; where there is a choice, the candidates do not explicitly offer alternative political positions.

Thus, in treating the USSR and eastern Europe as case studies of socialist economic performance, some care is required in distinguishing the inherent characteristics of a socialist economy from those which merely reflect the Soviet type of political system. Some authors have argued that the Soviet system has little to do with socialism, and merely aims to secure the privileges of a new bureaucratic exploitative class (for a recent statement of this line of thought, see Voslensky, 1984). Logically, this would suggest that few conclusions about socialism can be drawn from observation of eastern Europe.

This is a complex issue, but my own view is that this 'new bureaucratic class' analysis is mistaken. The privileges of the bureaucracy may be regarded as a natural extension of the widespread use of material incentives to reward desired forms of behaviour (it is not material incentives and inequality as such which are suspect in Soviet-type economies, but only market-related incentives). Although on occasions, as in the later Brezhnev era, these privileges may get out of control, the principle behind them is similar to the utilization of good pay and conditions of work to maintain the morale of the army and the police in the west: to reward key parts of the apparatus for their loyalty, precisely because otherwise they would have no great stake in the political system. Moreover the 'new ruling class' analysis seriously underestimates the role of ideology in the Soviet bloc. The attention given to ideological matters, the concern to recruit workers to the Communist Party and the tremendous political ferment caused by any overt signs of disaffection of the working class all serve as evidence that the dictum of the Communist Party as the party of the proletariat is taken seriously, and is not just a cover for bureaucratic rule.

Despite the privileges of the bureaucracy, economic arrangements suggest the same. Relative to capitalist countries on a similar level of development, it is the manual workers who emerge as the privileged class under Soviet socialism, because income distribution is more equal, the wage differential between manual and non-manual workers is small and employment is virtually guaranteed. These are the tangible benefits which the rulers seek to offer the manual workers in an effort to secure their allegiance to socialism in general and to the Soviet system in particular. Changes to the economic system which might undermine these advantages, for instance by widening income differentials or creating a threat of unemployment, are highly sensitive political issues in these countries, as advocates of reform are only too well aware.

Thus there seems little reason to treat evidence from eastern Europe as telling us nothing about 'true socialism', whatever that may be. Yet it is evident that political considerations have tended to circumscribe the degree to which east European countries have been able to break out of the Stalinist mould into which their economic structures were set in the years 1949 to 1953. A bureaucratic economic system is well suited to a political structure which confers omnipotence on the Communist Party. Officially the Communist Party exercises a 'leading role' in society. In practice this amounts to a right to oversee all activities and to veto any 'negative developments'. As Roy Medvedev (1977, p. xviii) has described it

> Virtually the entire economic and social life of our vast country is run from a single centre. The smallest organisation, even a club of dog-lovers or cactus-growers, is supervised by the appropriate body of the CPSU . . . Every aspect of a Soviet citizen's life is dependent on the actions of state and party bureaucrats who lose no opportunity to press the point home.

It is altogether more convenient if economic life operates according to similar principles. Thus if managers are always subordinate to the ministerial bureaucracy, they will be accustomed to obeying orders and it makes little difference whether these come from the Communist Party or state officials. If, however, managers did have important rights to take their own decisions and to ignore civil servants, as in a market system, they would quickly come into conflict with Communist Party functionaries. The Communist Party would have to recognize that some decisions were not subject to its veto. This is something which it has not been willing to accept.

Although the Yugoslav case demonstrates the possibility of other forms of economic organization in a one-party state, the history of the country suggests that it is very much a special case. Its institutional development seems to have been strongly influenced in a *negative* way by the Soviet experience, initially as part of an effort to consolidate political support in the face of Soviet hostility. It is extremely difficult to judge how much inherent stability there would be to a one-party state based on the ideology of self-management if the negative example of the Soviet bloc was not there to act as a damper on popular expectations and to propel the party leadership away from the centralist model.

There are certain economic phenomena in Soviet bloc countries which appear to be closely linked to the political system. The tendency towards the over-stretching of investment resources and for markets to be characterized by excess demand is one of them. This can be observed even in the Hungarian economy after the reform. In Yugoslavia, also, the authorities have displayed a strong bias towards a high investment rate, maintaining negative real interest rates to this end, but in the self-management system excess demand tends to be reflected in balance of payments crises more than in physical shortages.

The distinctive feature of the Soviet political system is the apparent omnipotence of the Communist Party within the state's borders. The political leadership thus faces no internal constraint on its power; overt political competition is entirely external. The desire to meet this external challenge creates a yearning for ambitious schemes of economic development. Since fundamental institutional change is out of the question, economic growth appears to depend largely on the resources devoted to it, or in other words on the rate of investment. Thus the weakness of internal political constraints induces a desire to maximize the investment rate, which tends to be pushed up as high as is consistent with internal political stability. Since this political bias towards high investment rates is known to the planners, they tend to authorize a volume of investment which on paper is consistent with macroeconomic balance, but which they know from past experience will in practice turn out to be excessive. In a political system where voters had the opportunity to remove their political leaders and replace them with others, this type of behaviour would undoubtedly be swiftly punished through the ballot box (it is probably significant that western politicians are never tempted to advocate price controls stringent enough to create the danger of shortages as a vote-catching anti-inflationary measure). Since political leaders in eastern Europe and the Soviet Union do not face this type of constraint, the economy is characterized by permanent excess demand in investment goods markets, and frequent shortages, even if not always a state of aggregate excess demand, in consumption goods markets.

The other major characteristic of these economies which I identified in earlier chapters was the softness of budget constraints. This results from extreme reluctance to penalize workers for the poor economic performance of their enterprises, and in particular, to use the threat of redundancy or bankruptcy to force through improvements. Though these sanctions exist in law, they are seldom applied, and the threat is known to be hollow. This creates acute difficulties in maintaining a satisfactory rate of technical progress, because the pressures on enterprises to improve their efficiency are gravely weakened.

This aspect of the economies of the Soviet bloc seems to me to reflect something quite fundamental in the thinking of the international socialist movement. In eastern Europe and the Soviet Union, soft budget constraints serve the important ideological function of removing the insecurity felt by large groups of workers under capitalism. Indeed, it was precisely the desire to achieve this by political ends that led to the creation of the socialist movement in the first place. Though a minority has always been influenced by Marxian ideas about the exploitative nature of capitalism, this view has never become the majority view in the west, where the energies of the movement have always been directed overwhelmingly to more immediate and less abstract concerns that reflect the vulnerability of those with a weak position in the labour market. Even demands for nationalization have arisen more from a concern for job security than from antipathy to private ownership as such, as is shown by the tendency for such demands to focus on weak and declining industries. At the risk of oversimplification, one might say that the socialist movement is the proletariat united against the uncertainty and adjustment costs of a market economy rather than against capitalist exploitation, and its ideology mirrors that. Its instinct is always to insure workers' incomes as far as possible. In a market economy this programme, if pushed far enough, can create problems of disincentives and rigidities that inhibit adjustment and impose losses on society as a whole.

Where a socialist ideology contains an additional Marxian component that sees socialism as a radically superior mode of production in which workers' interests are paramount, the political pressure for more or less complete insulation of workers' incomes from market forces becomes almost irresistible. This is exactly the situation in the Soviet bloc and Yugoslavia, where the result is soft budget constraints.

The whole issue of soft budget constraints is a difficult one for the socialist movement precisely because the movement is rooted in what are essentially trade union attitudes. Even its intellectual element tends to take on these attitudes in order to define itself in relation to other intellectuals. But trade union attitudes, as just explained, are in large degree reactions against the everyday behaviour of market forces, and in effect, against hard budget constraints. The only socialists who display any awareness that the softness of budget constraints is an intellectual and practical problem for the socialist economy are those who have studied its effects in the Soviet bloc, and it is notable that their practical proposals reveal a concern to avoid repetition of this mistake (Nove, 1983; Hare, 1985). Bruno Frey (1986) has recently lamented that only economists favour the price mechanism; one might paraphrase this and say that amongst socialists, only economists favour hard budget constraints.

The parallel is not exact, but it has some merits. Antipathy to the price mechanism derives essentially, in my opinion, from the potential redistributive effect of price changes. Since people tend to be risk averse, and *actual* costs are felt much more acutely than *opportunity* costs, fear of loss from price fluctuations predominates over the prospect of gain. Even where the direction of anticipated price movements is clear, a minority of losers concentrated in politically sensitive areas may be able to mount successful resistance to a change from which the majority would gain (the agricultural price support policy of the EEC is a classic case of this). The socialist movement's antipathy to hard budget constraints contains both these elements. Hard budget constraints threaten vulnerable groups of workers with loss of jobs or status; their advantages as a stimulant to technical progress are diffused throughout the population. Moreover these workers are easily organized as a pressure group through trade unions, and for ideological reasons this pressure group has particular influence in the socialist movement. Thus a concentrated, easily organized group which cannot avoid the risks associated with hard budget constraints (unlike entrepreneurs, who usually have options other than entrepreneurship) finds in the socialist movement a convenient vehicle for its opposition to them.

I would not wish to imply by this that the *electorate as a whole* is unaware of the advantages of hard budget constraints. Indeed I consider the opposite to be the case, and that this explains something which has always puzzled socialists in western Europe: the unpopularity of further nationalization, as revealed in repeated opinion polls since 1945, and the lack of opposition to privatization in more recent times. People know that private ownership of the means of production involves a certain cost to them in shareholders' dividend payments. They would be hard put to place a figure on this cost, but they tolerate it as long as private firms appear to be competitive and responsive to consumer interests, because their perception is that the losses resulting from reduced pressure to be efficient in monopolized nationalized industries are likely to be much greater. Capitalist income is viewed as a worthwhile price to pay for imposing competitive behaviour and hard budget constraints on producers.

To put it another way, the issue of the hardness of budget constraints is more fundamental in the public perception than the issue of ownership of the means of production. This would have surprised Marx, and probably reflects a combination of developments since his day: a long-run shift in labour market conditions in favour of workers, effective protective legislation for consumers and the increasingly institutional character of share ownership. The result has been to keep capitalist exploitation within bounds and to spotlight instead questions of efficiency and technical progress, which are perceived to be the major determinants of living standards over the medium term.

The Soviet bloc has been forced to face up to the implications of soft budget constraints by its weak economic performance in the post-1975 period. Its leaders have not only had to give up the goal of catching up with western Europe, but are increasingly aware that their economies have if anything been falling further behind. This is the economic reality behind Gorbachev's 'perestroika'. Unfortunately the negative aspect of this programme (the repudiation of the past) has so far been much clearer than its positive aspect. The traditional response of an investment drive now seems inadequate, and the accompanying squeeze on consumption might in any case create serious popular discontent. Some reform of the economic mechanism is indicated.

Accordingly more interest has recently been shown in the Hungarian experiment. Nevertheless there is obvious reluctance to imitate it. After two decades, it is reasonably clear that the advantages of the Hungarian system lie chiefly in areas to which the political leaders of the Soviet Union and eastern Europe attach low importance – the responsiveness of production to consumer demand – whilst in areas to which they attach high importance – especially technical progress and economic growth – its record has been decidedly mixed. Official growth figures probably have a greater 'real' content in Hungary, but since they have been generally unimpressive (especially in the 1980s), this in itself is not significant. I argued in chapter 6 that the principal reason for this was that the reform did not resolve the problem of soft budget constraints. This is not altogether surprising, for the softness of budget constraints encapsulates the twin axioms of political life in the Soviet bloc: paternalistic overseeing of producers by the party-state bureaucracy, and the security of employment and income. To overturn either one of these is difficult enough; to overturn them both appears well-nigh impossible without fundamental change, for which nothing less than the breaking of the political monopoly of the Communist Party would probably suffice.

Gorbachev has promoted a flowering of ideas for economic reform (for a survey, see Nove, 1987), and his chief advisers have given many signs that they would agree with much of the above analysis, yet comprehensive economic reform proposals have yet to be formulated. Indeed the whole political situation is in a constant state of flux, and by late 1987 the reform process was showing some signs of running into the sand. Gorbachev's speech on Soviet history ruled out any fundamental reinterpretations, continuing to present Stalin as the great defender of the 'correct' line in the 1920s, whilst at the same central committee meeting Boris Yeltsin, the Moscow Party Secretary, was ostentatiously dismissed for excessive reforming zeal. The possibility of bankruptcies is being widely canvassed in the USSR and a number of east European countries, but the whole programme of economic reform now looks fragile and vulnerable to any decisive, even if only local, display of worker discontent. This would give the opponents of change the ammunition they need to argue that reform would drive a wedge between party and working class.

The fundamental issue here is that bankruptcies and the appearance of unemployment on any significant scale threaten the delicate ideological structure of society built up over decades. Workers would regard it as the antithesis of planning and the return of the insecurities associated with capitalism, whilst the inability of local Communist Party functionaries to prevent these occurrences would rend the web of patronage by which they establish their legitimacy. The Communist Party would lose face, and its claims to a leading role in society would be seriously undermined. Thus major economic changes almost certainly require the ending of the Communist Party's political monopoly. But no Communist Party leader could seriously propose this without committing political suicide, and Gorbachev certainly is not doing so, whatever grand phrases about democracy he may offer.

Thus it is hard to envisage by what route major changes could come about in the political and economic life of the Soviet bloc countries, despite the widespread malaise that obviously exists. The existing system has a logical consistency which reforms inevitably disrupt. For this reason, so long as economic performance is not transparently bad and living standards continue on a modest upward path, these countries will probably undergo only limited change in the remainder of the twentieth century.

On the other hand, if the analysis given above is correct, it is difficult to foresee a radical transformation of multi-party democracies into socialist economies either. People have had enough experience of government intervention to know that the politicization of economic decisions creates rigidities which often have large economic costs. To avoid this, they will vote to preserve a market system, without being too concerned about whether firms are in private or public ownership, relying on competition, taxation and anti-monopoly legislation to keep capitalist incomes in proportion, whilst themselves receiving an increasing share of it through their pension funds and other institutional investments. In essence what I am saying is that the average member of the population is aware, from casual observation, of the connections between hard budget constraints and economic progress, and will not lightly risk these advantages by voting for a drastic increase in public ownership. Although in theory publicly-owned firms *can* compete vigorously against one another, the critical point is that there is no guarantee that the government will not succumb to political pressures to soften budget constraints and permit collusion between them. To restrict the size of the public sector represents an insurance against this.

Bibliography

Adam, J. 1976: Systems of wage regulation in the Soviet bloc. *Soviet Studies*, 28, 91–109.

Amann, R., Cooper, J., and Davies, R.W. 1977: *The Technological Level of Soviet Industry*. London: Yale University Press.

Ascherson, N. 1981: *The Polish August*. Harmondsworth: Penguin.

Ash, T.G. 1983: *The Polish Revolution: Solidarity 1980–82*. London: Jonathan Cape.

Askanas, B., and Levcik, F. 1983: The dispersion of wages in the sumption in Poland and Austria. *Journal of Comparative Economics*, 9, 164–77.

Askanas, B., and Levcik, F. 1983: The dispersion of wages in the CMEA countries (including a comparison with Austria). In S. Frowen (ed.), *Controlling Industrial Economies*, London: Macmillan, 193–230.

Bajt, A. 1971: Investment cycles in European socialist economies: a review article. *Journal of Economic Literature*, 9, 53–63.

Balassa, B., and Tyson, L.D'A. 1986: Policy responses to external shocks in Hungary and Yugoslavia 1974–6 and 1979–81. In US Congress Joint Economic Committee (1986), 1, 57–80.

Bauer, T. 1978: Investment cycles in planned economies. *Acta Oeconomica*, 21, 243–60.

Bergson, A. 1961: *The Real National Income of Soviet Russia since 1928*. Cambridge, Mass.: Harvard University Press.

Bergson, A. and Levine, H.S. 1983: *The Soviet Economy: Towards the Year 2000*. London: Allen and Unwin.

Bergson, A. 1984: Income inequality under Soviet socialism. *Journal of Economic Literature*, 22, 1052–99.

Bergson, A. 1987: On Soviet real investment growth. *Soviet Studies*, 39, 406–24.

Berliner, J. 1976: *The Innovation Decision in Soviet Industry*. Cambridge, Mass.: MIT Press.

Birman, I. 1978: From the achieved level. *Soviet Studies*, 30, 153–72.

Blackaby, F.T. (ed.) 1978: *British Economic Policy 1960–74: Demand Management*. Cambridge: National Institute of Economic Research.

Bleaney, M.F. 1987: Disequilibrium macroeconometrics in centrally planned economies: are the results biased? *University of Nottingham Department of Economics*, mimeo.

Bornstein, M. 1985: Improving the Soviet economic mechanism. *Soviet Studies*, 37, 1–30.

Bromke, A., and Strong, J.W. (eds) 1973: *Gierek's Poland*. New York: Praeger.

Brus, W. 1982: Aims, methods and political determinants of the economic policy of Poland, 1970–1980. Chapter 4 of A. Nove et al. (1982).

Brus, W. 1986: Chapters 23 to 26 of M. Kaser (ed.), *An Economic History of Eastern Europe 1919–75*, Oxford: Clarendon Press.

Cameron, N.E. 1981: Economic growth in the USSR, Hungary, and East and West Germany. *Journal of Comparative Economics*, 5, 24–42.

Carr, E.H. 1966: *The Bolshevik Revolution 1917–1923* 3 vols. Baltimore: Penguin.

Carr, E.H. 1969: *The Interregnum 1923–1924*. Baltimore: Penguin.

Carr, E.H. 1970: *Socialism in One Country 1924–1926* 3 vols. Baltimore: Penguin.

Chapman, J.G. 1963: Consumption. In A. Bergson and S. Kuznets (eds), *Economic Trends in the Soviet Union*, Cambridge, Mass.: Harvard University Press, 235–82.

Charques, R. 1958: *The Twilight of Imperial Russia*. London: Phoenix House.

Clarke, R.A., and Matko, D.J.I. 1983: *Soviet Economic Facts, 1917–81*. London: Macmillan.

Crisp, O. 1976: *Studies in the Russian Economy before 1914*. London: Macmillan.

Daniel, Z. 1985: The effect of housing allocation on social inequality in Hungary. *Journal of Comparative Economics*, 9, 391–409.

Dyker, D. 1983: *The Process of Investment in the Soviet Union*. Cambridge: Cambridge University Press.

Ellman, M. 1986: The macro-economic situation in the USSR – retrospect and prospect. *Soviet Studies*, 38, 530–42.

Falkus, M.E. 1972: *The Industrialization of Russia, 1700–1914*. London: Allen and Unwin.

Fallenbuchl, Z.M. 1977: The Polish economy in the 1970s. In US Congress Joint Economic Committee (1977).

Falus-Szikra, K. 1986: Wage and income disparities between the first and second economies in Hungary. *Acta Oeconomica*, 36, 91–103.

Faluvégi, L. 1986: The Seventh Five-Year Plan of the Hungarian economy (for 1986–1990). *Acta Oeconomica*, 36, 3–19.

Fejtö, F. 1971: *A History of the People's Democracies*. London: Pall Mall.

Frey, B.S. 1986: Economists favour the price mechanism – who else does? *Kyklos*, 39, 537–63.

Gagnon, V.P. Jr 1987: Gorbachev and the collective contract brigade. *Soviet Studies*, 39, 1–23.

Gerschenkron, A. 1965: Agrarian policies and industrialization: Russia 1861–1917. Ch. 8 of H.J. Habbakuk and M. Postan (eds), *The Cambridge Economic History of Europe* Vol. 6 Part II, Cambridge: Cambridge University Press.

Goldsmith, R.W. 1961: The economic growth of Tsarist Russia 1860–1913. *Economic Development and Cultural Change*, 9, 441–75.

Gomulka, S., and Rostowski, J. 1984: The reformed Polish economic system 1982–1983. *Soviet Studies*, 36, 386–405.

Gomulka, S. 1986: *Growth, Innovation and Reform in Eastern Europe*. Brighton: Wheatsheaf.

Granick, D. 1975: *Enterprise Guidance in Eastern Europe: A Comparison of Four Socialist Economies*. Princeton, N.J.: Princeton University Press.

Hall, J.B. 1986: Plan bargaining in the Hungarian economy: an interview with Dr Laszlo Antal. *Comparative Economic Studies*, 28 (2), 49–58.

Hanson, P. 1983: Success indicators revisited: the July 1979 Soviet decree on planning and management. *Soviet Studies*, 35, 1–13.

Hanson, P. 1984: The CIA, the TsSU and the real growth of Soviet investment. *Soviet Studies*, 36, 571–81.

Hare, P.G. 1981: Aggregate planning by means of input-output and material-balances systems. *Journal of Comparative Economics*, 5, 272–91.

Hare, P.G. 1983: The beginnings of institutional reform in Hungary. *Soviet Studies*, 35, 313–30.

Hare, P.G. 1985: *Planning the British Economy*. London: Macmillan.

Havlik, P. 1985: A comparison of purchasing power parity and consumption levels in Austria and Czechoslovakia. *Journal of Comparative Economics*, 9, 178–90.

Holzman, F.D. 1986: Further thoughts on the significance of Soviet subsidies to eastern Europe. *Comparative Economic Studies*, 27, 59–65.

Howard, D.H. 1976: A note on hidden inflation in the Soviet Union. *Soviet Studies*, 28, 599–608.

Illés, I. 1986: Structural change in the Hungarian economy (1979–1985). *Acta Oeconomica*, 36, 21–33.

Jasny, N. 1949: *The Socialized Agriculture of the USSR*. Stanford: Stanford University Press.

Kapitány, Z., Kornai, J., and Szabó, J. 1984: Reproduction of shortage in the Hungarian car market. *Soviet Studies*, 36, 236–56.

Kenedi, J. 1981: *Do it Yourself: Hungary's Hidden Economy*. London: Pluto Press.

Kende, P., and Strmiska, Z. 1984: *Egalité et Inégalités en Europe de l'Est*. Paris: Presses de la Fondation Nationale des Sciences Politiques.

Kendrick, J.W. 1961: *Productivity Trends in the United States*. New York: National Bureau of Economic Research.

Keren, M. 1973: The new economic system in the GDR: an obituary. *Soviet Studies*, 24, 554–87.

Keren, M. 1977: The return of the ancien régime: the GDR in the 1970s. In US Congress Joint Economic Committee (1977), 720–65.

Keren, M. 1987: Consumer prices in the GDR since 1950: the construction of price indices from purchasing power parities. *Soviet Studies*, 39, 247–68.

Kornai, J. 1959: *Overcentralization in Economic Administration*. Oxford: Oxford University Press.

Kornai, J. 1980: *Economics of Shortage* 2 vols. Amsterdam: North-Holland.

Kornai, J. 1982: *Growth, Shortage and Efficiency: A Macrodynamic Model of the Socialist Economy*. Oxford: Basil Blackwell.

Kornai, J., and Matits, A. 1984: Softness of the budget constraint – an analysis relying on data of firms. *Acta Oeconomica*, 32, 223–49.

Kornai, J. 1986: The Hungarian reform process: visions, hopes and reality. *Journal of Economic Literature*, 24, 1687–737.

Köves, A. 1986: Foreign economic equilibrium, economic development and economic policy in the CMEA countries. *Acta Oeconomica*, 36, 35–53.

Kushnirsky, F.I. 1982: *Soviet Economic Planning 1965–80*. Boulder, Col.: Westview Press.

Laky, T. 1980: The hidden mechanism of recentralization in Hungary. *Acta Oeconomica*, 24, 95–109.

Lazarcik, G. 1986: Comparative growth of agricultural output, inputs and productivity in eastern Europe, 1965–82. In US Congress Joint Economic Committee (1986), 1, 388–425.

Lewis, A. 1978: *Growth and Fluctuations, 1870–1913*. London: Allen and Unwin.

Lydall, H.F. 1968: *The Structure of Earnings*. Oxford: Oxford University Press.

Lydall, H.F. 1984: *Yugoslav Socialism: Theory and Practice*. Oxford: Oxford University Press.

Maddison, A. 1969: *Economic Growth in Japan and the USSR*. London: Allen and Unwin.

Malafayev, A.N. 1964: *Istoriya Tsenoobrazovaniya v SSSR, 1917–1963gg*. Moscow: Izdatel'stvo Sozial'no-ekonomicheskoi Literaturi "Mysl'".

Marer, P. 1986: Economic reform in Hungary: from central planning to regulated market. In US Congress Joint Economic Committee (1986), 3, 223–97.

Mason, D.S. 1985. *Public Opinion and Political Change in Poland, 1980–82*. Cambridge: Cambridge University Press.

Medvedev, R. 1977: *On Socialist Democracy*. Nottingham: Spokesman.

Michal, J.M. 1978: Size distribution of household incomes and earnings in developed socialist countries. In W. Krelle and A.F. Shorrocks (eds), *Personal Income Distribution*, Amsterdam: North-Holland.

Moorsteen, R.H., and Powell, R.P. 1966: *The Soviet Capital Stock, 1928–62*. Homewood, Illinois: Irwin.

Nove, A. 1977: *The Soviet Economic System*. London: Allen and Unwin.

Nove, A. 1981: Note on growth, investment and price indices. *Soviet Studies*, 33, 142–5.

Nove, A. 1982: *An Economic History of the USSR*. Harmondsworth: Penguin.

Nove, A., Höhmann, H.H., and Seidenstrecher, G. 1982: *The East European Economies in the 1970s*. London: Butterworth.

Nove, A. 1983: *The Economics of Feasible Socialism*. London: Allen and Unwin.

Nove, A. 1987: 'Radical reform': problems and prospects. *Soviet Studies*, 39, 1–23.

Nutter, G.W. 1962: *Growth of Industrial Production in the Soviet Union*, Princeton, N.J.: Princeton University Press.

OECD [Organisation for Economic Co-operation and Development] *Economic Survey of Yugoslavia* (annual publication). Paris: OECD.

Portes, R. 1977: Hungary's economic performance, policy and prospects. In US Congress Joint Economic Committee (1977), 766–815.

Portes, R., and Winter, D. 1980: Disequilibrium estimates for consumption goods markets in centrally planned economies. *Review of Economic Studies*, 57, 137–59.

Prout, C. 1985: *Market Socialism in Yugoslavia*. Oxford: Oxford University Press.

Pryor, F. 1977: Some costs and benefits of markets. *Quarterly Journal of Economics*, 91, 81–102.

Quandt, R.E., Portes, R., Winter, D., and Yeo, S. 1987: Macroeconomic planning and disequilibrium: estimates for Poland, 1955–80. *Econometrica*, 55, 19–41.

Révész, G. 1986: On the expansion and functioning of the direct market sector of the Hungarian economy. *Acta Oeconomica*, 36, 105–21.

Robinson, W.F. 1973: *The Pattern of Reform in Hungary: A Political, Economic and Cultural Analysis*, New York: Praeger.

Rusinow, D. 1977: *The Yugoslav Experiment*. London: C. Hurst and Co.

Sanford, G. 1984: The Polish Communist leadership and the onset of the state of war. *Soviet Studies*, 36, 494–512.

Schroeder, G.E. 1982: Soviet economic 'reform' decrees: more steps on the treadmill. In US Congress Joint Economic Committee, *Soviet Economy in the 1980s: Problems and Prospects*, Washington: US Government Printing Office, Part I, 65–88.

Smith, A.H. 1983: *The Planned Economies of Eastern Europe*. London: Croom Helm.

Spulber, N. 1957: *The Economies of Communist Eastern Europe*. Cambridge, Mass.: MIT Press.

Staniszkis, J. 1984: *Poland's Self-limiting Revolution*. Princeton, N.J.: Princeton University Press.

Steiner, J.E. 1982: Disguised inflation in Soviet industry. *Journal of Comparative Economics*, 6, 278–87.

Szelenyi, I. 1983: *Urban Inequalities under State Socialism*. Oxford: Oxford University Press.

Tretyakova, A., and Birman, I. 1976: Input-output analysis in the USSR. *Soviet Studies*, 28, 157–86.

Turcan, J.R. 1977: Some observations on retail distribution in Poland. *Soviet Studies*, 29, 128–36.

Tyson, L. D'A. 1977: Liquidity crises in the Yugoslav economy: an alternative to bankruptcy. *Soviet Studies*, 29, 284–95.

UNECE [United Nations Economic Commission for Europe] *Economic Survey of Europe* (annual publication). Geneva: United Nations.

United States Congress Joint Economic Committee 1977: *East European Economies post-Helsinki*. Washington: US Government Printing Office.

United States Congress Joint Economic Committee 1986: *East European Economies: Slow Growth in the 1980s* 3 vols. Washington: US Government Printing Office.

Vajna, T. 1982: Problems and trends in the development of the Hungarian New Economic Mechanism: a balance sheet of the 1970s. Chapter 6 of A. Nove et al. (1982).

Voslensky, M. 1984: *Nomenklatura: Anatomy of the Soviet Ruling Class*. London: Bodley Head.

Wädekin, K.-E. 1982: *Agrarian Policies in Communist Europe*. The Hague: Martinus Nijhoff.
Walker, M. 1986: *The Waking Giant: the Soviet Union in the Gorbachev era*. London: Michael Joseph.
Wiles, P.J.D., and Markowski, S. 1971: Income distribution under capitalism and communism: some facts about Poland, the UK, the USA and the USSR. *Soviet Studies*, 22, 344–69 and 487–571.
Wiles, P.J.D. 1978: Our shaky data base. In W. Krelle and A.F. Shorrocks (eds), *Personal Income Distribution*, Amsterdam: North-Holland.
Wiles, P.J.D. 1982: Soviet consumption and investment prices, and the meaningfulness of real investment. *Soviet Studies*, 34, 289–95.
Winiecki, J. 1985: Portes ante portas: a critique of the revisionist interpretation of inflation under central planning. *Comparative Economic Studies*, 27 (2), 25–51.
Winiecki, J. 1986: Are Soviet-type economies entering an era of long-term decline? *Soviet Studies*, 38, 325–48.
Zaleski, E. 1962: *Planification de la Croissance, et Fluctuations Economiques en U.R.S.S., 1918–1932*. Vol. 1. Paris: Société d'Edition d'Enseignement Supérieur.
Zaleski, E., et al. 1969: *Science Policy in the USSR*. Paris: OECD.
Zaleski, E. 1980: *Stalinist Planning for Economic Growth, 1933–52*. London: Macmillan.
Zielinski, J. 1973: *Economic Reforms in Polish Industry*. Oxford: Oxford University Press.

Index